YO-AFJ-557

PERGAMON INTERNATIONAL LIBRARY
of Science, Technology, Engineering and Social Studies
*The 1000-volume original paperback library in aid of education,
industrial training and the enjoyment of leisure*

Publisher: Robert Maxwell, M.C.

P52

POVERTY:
WEALTH OF MANKIND

SYSTEMS SCIENCE AND WORLD ORDER LIBRARY
General Editor: Ervin Laszlo

Explorations of World Order

LASZLO, E. & BIERMAN, J.
Goals in a Global Community
Volume I: Studies in the Conceptual Foundations
Volume II: The International Values and Goals Studies

LASZLO, E.
The Inner Limits of Mankind:
Heretical Reflections on Today's Values, Culture and Politics

GIARINI, O. & LOUBERGE, H.
The Diminishing Returns to Technology
An Essay on the Crisis in Economic Growth

Innovations in Systems Science
IN PREPARATION

LAVIOLETTE, P. A. (ed.)
Systems Anthropology. Selected Papers by Ludwig von Bertalanffy

GEYER, F. R.
Alienation and General Systems Theory

POVERTY:
WEALTH OF MANKIND

BY

ALBERT TÉVOÉDJRÈ

Director, International Institute for Labour Studies,
Geneva, Switzerland
Deputy Director-General, International Labour Office

Foreword by

Jan Tinbergen and Dom Helder Camara

PERGAMON PRESS

OXFORD · NEW YORK · TORONTO · SYDNEY · PARIS · FRANKFURT

U.K.	Pergamon Press Ltd., Headington Hill Hall, Oxford OX3 0BW, England
U.S.A.	Pergamon Press Inc., Maxwell House, Fairview Park, Elmsford, New York 10523, U.S.A.
CANADA	Pergamon of Canada Ltd., 75 The East Mall, Toronto, Ontario, Canada
AUSTRALIA	Pergamon Press (Aust.) Pty. Ltd., P.O. Box 544, Potts Point, N.S.W. 2011, Australia.
FRANCE	Pergamon Press SARL, 24 rue des Ecoles, 75240 Paris, Cedex 05, France
FEDERAL REPUBLIC OF GERMANY	Pergamon Press GmbH, 6242 Kronberg-Taunus, Pferdstrasse 1, Federal Republic of Germany

British Library Cataloguing in Publication Data

Tévoédjrè, Albert
Poverty, wealth of mankind.—(Systems science and world order library).—
(Pergamon international library).
1. Economic development
I. Title II. Series
330.9   HD82   78-40632

ISBN 0-08-023367-8 (Hard cover)
ISBN 0-08-023366-X (Flexicover)

Printed in Great Britain by
William Clowes & Sons Limited
London, Beccles and Colchester

THIS BOOK

the proceeds of its copyrights to be used to support
the programmes on "new forms of solidarity" undertaken by the
International Institute for Labour Studies

is dedicated
to my sons:
Jacques,
Christian,
Eric,

And to everyone of their generation who shares their hopes,
So that they may carry on the task that has been started
And give new life to the words of the oath sworn by Franz Fanon,
this young man for all seasons:

> *"As a man I undertake to face up to the*
> *risk of being destroyed in order that*
> *two or three truths may shed their essential*
> *Light on the world."*

Geneva, 8 September 1977   A. T.

Contents

Contents

Foreword

In this book the Director of the International Institute for Labour Studies tackles some of the great questions confronting the world today, particularly at this time when we are becoming conscious of certain "limits to growth", the term employed in the Meadows' report. On page 131 the author himself says "It is not the purpose of this work to analyse the forms and nature of new international relations needed to establish the new order so much talked of today." I personally view it as a philosophical study of many of the aspects of development, a study undertaken by an author of genuine African culture who has a rich and wide experience of Western and especially French culture.

The title, *Poverty: Wealth of Mankind*, may at first appear to be a paradox; in fact it expresses exactly the central thesis of the book, which, if I may state it in my own way, shows how simplicity of life-style constitutes the very purpose of individual and social development. What we loosely call poverty is in fact destitution, which both the author and I of course violently abhor. The other imperative which he highlights is the need for solidarity. Here again I am in complete agreement with him.

Mr. Tévoédjrè devotes a large part of his plea for simplicity of life-style to decrying the cult of opulence, a characteristic of the way of life adopted by so very many Westerners as well as by some of the people who took over their top positions in their former colonies—"the indigenous notables" (p. 40). He shows to what extent the availability of surplus possessions intoxicates our societies, and how our present-day restlessness has made of time or leisure for reflection a "rare commodity", while the big cities are becoming veritable cancers (p. 49). In the West, for instance, many of us, including myself, are only too aware of the increasing difficulty of bringing up children, since their access to money and material goods makes it quite impossible for their parents to impose some form of punishment for bad behaviour.

Mr. Tévoédjrè calls upon the peoples of the Third World to base their thinking and their efforts on inductive reasoning, that is to say on the experience and realities of their own lives, rather than on abstract principles adopted from the industrialized countries and generally unsuited to their own surroundings. He recommends "internal mobilization" as offering grounds for some hope in the light of appropriate experience gained in China and Japan. He also refers to Western youth's search for a different kind of life. In all this there are many points where I share his reasoning.

But, as is so often the case, the more one reflects the more new problems come to light: this is precisely what enhances human thinking and keeps our minds alert. I would like to cite a few examples to illustrate my meaning.

The first problem to be considered concerns the point beyond which simplicity yields to the useless and the superfluous. Every Western or urban society is in my opinion not an evil *per se*. Besides, modern industry has provided a number of services for mankind: one need but mention a few minor items at random like electric light, the vacuum cleaner, public transport or drip-dry shirts. All these help people to have more time for reading, education or creative work. On the other hand it is true that modern society encourages some people to raid post offices and the question is where to seek the root of this mischief and of all the derailments of Western society. Pursuing Mr. Tévoédjrè's thinking, it can be stated that lack of solidarity with children, as shown by the alarming rise in the number of divorces, is largely responsible for their conduct in later years.

Recognizing that the very large cities have gradually become hotbeds of all manner of deplorable social behaviour, we find ourselves confronted by another question, the complexity of which is well known: what is in fact the ideal size for a city?

Similarly, I agree with the author that too many private cars constitutes an obstacle to public transport. This raises the delicate problem of determining just who is entitled to own a car, and who is not.

I am also prepared to follow his reasoning when he gives an exact description of the terrible conditions under which many of those who have become "superfluous" in the rural areas are now obliged to "live" in the cities, or rather in hovels in the slums. Isn't part of the problem the excessively rapid growth of the population? Shouldn't the public health measures introduced by the World Health Organization in a number of developing countries have been accompanied from the start by a policy of family planning, in other words of "spacing out births"?

Finally, the author sees a ray of hope in the attitude of young people in the rich countries. But I would add that there are social differences among youth in the West. Some groups do indeed show us a fine example of seeking a life of simplicity and human values; unfortunately there are others involved in violence and crime whose conduct can only be described as inhuman.

This book focuses our full attention on the most alarming realities of our Western society. It very rightly calls upon us to become aware of those realities, to reason inductively from this starting point and thus to think of how to get rid of them. This is an immensely complex challenge. I can testify that Albert Tévoédjrè makes us fully aware of the over-riding priority of that challenge.

JAN TINBERGEN

Preface

This book of Albert Tévoédjrè's does more than give us great hopes: it brings immense joy.

What a joy it is to see the peoples of Africa, Asia and Latin America making the same discoveries, which are of the greatest significance for their future.

As they embark on the experience of political independence, those peoples, who cannot always be identified with their present rulers, have to face up to a series of challenges:

the challenge of avoiding the terrible ambiguity of idealizing that consumer society which unbridled profit-making turns into a hell on earth and which is already rightly called a society of waste and suicide;

the challenge of knowing how to distinguish intelligently between repulsive and inadmissible destitution and the poverty which, properly conceived and lived, can and must be the Wealth of Mankind;

the challenge of always remaining alert in the face of the temptation of ridiculous mimicry which leads to imitating the political forms of the wealthy countries while forgetting and scorning that cultural identity which is so essential;

the challenge of substituting, to a greater and greater extent, the exchange of technology for the unacceptable and dangerous transfer of technology;

the challenge of resisting the mirage of massive industrialization which is so largely responsible for the spreading urban gangrene in developing countries, and also of resisting the formation of alliances between multinational corporations and privileged national groups, which by practising a form of veritable colonialism promote the setting up of investment paradises and the resulting rise of these countries' foreign indebtedness to unbearable levels.

Faced with these challenges, the peoples of the Third World can embark on such novel experiences as:

the experience of setting out courageously to re-invent an economic system by complementing the market economy with a service economy, by correcting such partial and deceptive indices as the gross national product index by means of indices of public well-being, which call for institutional reforms whereby the incredible differences in income levels found in most developing countries can be avoided;

the experience of discovering that the superpowers, which claim to be seeking to help the Third World, are in fact incapable of doing so without ulterior motives, since their aid leaves the imprint of an unduly heavy-handed presence almost equivalent to a new colonialism;

the experience of discovering that, as a popular Brazilian song suggests, "our world will be a better place when the least among us, who toils, believes in the least";

the experience of discovering that the only way out of the dilemma brought on by "robotizing and robot-making" projects drawn up in supertechnicians' offices is to replace them with projects on a human scale: that human scale which makes it possible for people to participate effectively in preparing, launching, carrying out and supervising projects where each individual is conscious of his dignity in the ranks of society.

All this and much more is to be seen and discerned in Albert Tévoédjrè's book, yet the text never wanders or becomes "vague". It takes on form and purpose in the "Solidarity Contract". There is a feeling that decisive steps are being taken. We will no longer be able to claim with any honesty that by aspiring to a world where we can breathe more easily (*Conviviality* by Ivan Illich, and *Project Hope*, by Roger Garaudy) we are getting lost in the stratosphere.

Admittedly we still have a long way to go: we have to make the small local communities ever more numerous in both developing and industrialized countries aware and eager to help create a more just and more human World.

Are we still dreaming? Are we still living in a complete Utopia? In Brazil our people sing,

"When we dream alone, it is just a dream.
When we dream together, it's the dawn of reality."

+ HELDER CAMARA
Archbishop of Olinda and Recife

CHAPTER I

Dethroning Money

The lion that kills is the lion that does not roar. He is like money, which strangles us without noise.

Tswana proverb
(Western Transvaal)

I loathe with all my heart this mad desire to eliminate distance and time, to increase our animal appetites and to go to the end of the world to satisfy them.

(Paraphrased from Gandhi)

One morning in January 1976 I received a telegram from Moshoeshoe II, King of Lesotho, inviting me to take part in a conference on international development at Maseru with Ivan Illich, Harry Oppenheimer and Judith Hart.

After much hesitation—these conferences are so numerous and sometimes quite meaningless—I let myself be persuaded, in the hope of helping to forward some ideas I believe in and, even more, of learning something new. (En route, I should have to stop over for the first time at Johannesburg, an unusual experience for a black African like me.)

Among the things I learnt was how dependent Lesotho was on South Africa. One evening, during a reception at the home of the Prime Minister, Dr. Jonathan Lebua, held in honour of Mr. A. Jumbe, First Vice-President of Tanzania, all the lights went out at the very moment when the Prime Minister of Lesotho was starting his official address to his guest. The blackout lasted the whole evening—an evening during which anything, even a kidnapping or a *coup d'Etat*, might have happened. In reply to my question, a guest sitting beside me explained that in Lesotho, electricity was supplied by a power-station outside the country, on South African territory, since they could not afford a modern generator at Maseru.

1

On the following day, I had to open a discussion on co-operation at the conference to which I had been invited. After having slept on the question, I decided to talk about poverty, to give a clearer and fuller definition of it, and to denounce the method of growth generally adopted, which makes us increasingly dependent on others. I was uneasy about this approach, for I did not know how the audience would react.

My speech, however, was so well received that I myself was surprised. After the discussion, Ivan Illich took me by the arm and said: "You should go more fully into what you have just been saying and write a book. Your idea is important."

His advice remained in my mind. I have since taken advantage of various lectures given as part of my activities in the International Institute for Labour Studies to pursue this line of thought, which has led me to affirm that poverty can be a form of wealth for mankind. This may seem surprising, but I propose to show that the paradox is only apparent.

Removing the paradox: a new look at poverty

Let me start by eliminating what is unnecessary and useless: the poverty that means indigence and destitution. I am no stranger to this kind of poverty, for I have known it in my own life.

I have lived it among my own people and I have surmounted it only thanks to the exceptional courage of my mother and the deep wisdom of my father—and also to a certain missionary sent by Providence who was good to us and made me start to think. To me as a young man it was the meeting of Persius with Cornutus as recounted in *L'Enfant d'Agrigente*.[1]

This introduction is intended simply to show that fatal famine, tropical diseases, permanent unemployment, beggary, ignorance, the cramped cabin where man and beast are crowded together, all this— which is called poverty, but which I call misery and destitution—all this is familiar to me. I think, then, that I know the nature and aim of the battle for development.

[1] A. J. Festugière: *L'enfant d'Agrigente* (Paris, Editions du Cerf, 1950).

The reader will no doubt realize that I am choosing deliberately to contribute to the rehabilitation of poverty, to its being regarded no longer as a fault but as a positive value.

Anyone willing to follow this line of thought will find that there is no lack of arguments to justify my choice.

All good dictionaries testify that "poor" also means "having only just what is necessary" or "having what is essential but no more".

It is this definition that I adopt and would like to highlight. The Littré supports me and this is confirmed by hundreds of other authorities such as the Webster,[2] which quotes the well-known words of R. A. Schermerhorn: "In poverty, morality and even a touch of happiness was possible, never in destitution."

To reinforce these scholastic definitions I shall refer to various ideas, thoughts and attitudes that can be found throughout the history, literature and books of wisdom of the whole world.

Albert Gelin,[3] in considering the Judeo-Christian tradition, distinguishes three attitudes:

—the approach that regards poverty as an outrage and sees the pauper as a pitiable victim;

—that which identifies the state of poverty with the state of sin and maintains that riches are one of the clearest indications of the sanction rewarding the righteous on earth;

—lastly, that which concerns us here and might be described as the happy medium:

... give me neither poverty nor riches; feed me with food convenient for me: lest I be full, and deny thee, and say "Who is the Lord?" or lest I be poor, and steal, and take the name of my God in vain.[4]

Looking through the many anthologies of Jewish thought, and in particular that of Edmond Fleg, reflections on the subject of poverty stand out as a constant theme. One name should, in my opinion, be singled out, that of Moses ben Maimon, known as Maimonides.

[2] *Webster's Third New International Dictionary.*

[3] See A. Gelin: *Les pauvres de Yahvé* (Paris, Editions du Cerf, 1953).

[4] Proverbs xxx. 8-9.

From Cordova to Cairo and Fez, Maimonides showed himself to be a profound and brilliant thinker, and was one of the most heeded spokesmen of a community severely tried by persecution and exile.

It is enough to recall one of his most outstanding books, *The Guide for the Perplexed*, where we can find the basic idea that the only factor common to all mankind is human dignity. In the Jewish tradition, this has led to the fusion of two generally separate concepts, justice and charity, into a single one: the economic solidarity designated by the word *"tzedakah"*. The idea that the rich must give part of their surplus to the poor was not a mere recommendation but a moral obligation, which in our times has become law in the form of income tax. Elsewhere (in his *Treatise Zeraïm*), Maimonides makes it clear that the purpose of *tzedakah* is to create anew a society where destitution has been overcome and that it manifests itself in forms of very different value. He thus distinguishes eight degrees of *tzedakah*, the lowest being to give reluctantly and the highest being to obtain work for a poor person or to let him share in your own activities so that he can avoid falling back into need.[5]

The other positive sense of poverty is to be found again in the many texts by which Denis de Rougemont is so well inspired when he writes: "The culture of Israel is poor by very reason of its purity. Its poverty may be regarded as its greatness. For that which is great is that which gives fullness. It is not riches but fidelity."[6]

The truth is that it is essential to recall things that everyone knows but that are lost in the graveyard of oblivion, whether deliberately or not: the Book of Job, the Magnificat, the Beatitudes in Saint Matthew, and also in Saint Luke, where the expression is perhaps more incisive.[7] It must be emphasized that the idea of a God who brings down the great and raises the meek is also to be found in the myths and the sacred writings of all the neighbouring countries of Israel and can be observed even earlier in Greco-Roman literature.

[5] See L. Stoleru: *Vaincre la pauvreté dans les pays riches* (Paris, Flammarion, 1974), p. 218.

[6] Denis de Rougemont: *Penser avec les mains* (Paris, Gallimard, 1972), p. 63.

[7] "Woe unto you that are rich!" (Luke vi. 24). This is expanded by Saint James, who writes: "Go to now, ye rich, weep and howl for your miseries that are coming upon you . . . the hire of the labourers . . . which is of you kept back by fraud, crieth out" (James v. 2, 4).

This last is full of judgements and counsels that strengthen our thesis. Let us take Horace and consider his "aurea mediocritas" (the golden mean)—or again his maxim: "True wisdom consists in wearing clothes and shoes that fit."

This theme crops up in the writing of all the ancients of the West, of every school, from Heraclitus to Seneca, from Plutarch to Virgil.

Nearer our own time, Bossuet recalls the attitude of the Romans when he writes: "Poverty was no evil for them. On the contrary, they regarded it as a means of keeping their freedom more intact, for they held nothing freer, nothing more independent than a man who could live on little."

Still more recently, Proudhon sets up poverty as a source of truth and happiness: "Poverty is seemly—her garments are not full of holes like the cynic's coat, her dwelling is clean, healthy and homely . . . She is neither pale nor hungry. Like Daniel's companions she is radiant with health as she eats her pulse; she receives her daily bread, she is content. Poverty is good, and we must consider her the principle of our joy."[8]

Here I should like also to mention Waldo, who was declared to be a heretic, but whose sect, the Waldenses, gave the highest value to "the outstanding dignity of the poor". This brings us close to Francis of Assisi, who at the same period was glorifying nature and extolling the brotherhood of the humble.

The illusions of property

Some wise men have been struck in particular by the harm caused by wealth, which is a source of envy that leads to poverty being seen as privation, the negative image of poverty conceived as a positive value, as it is understood here.

We can thus come back to Bossuet, putting his finger on an illogicality that he described at the time as new:

"The World now knows a certain fictitious charity . . . which

---

[8] Illich takes up the same idea when he recalls the notion of austerity as defined by Thomas Aquinas: "A virtue that does not exclude all pleasures, but only those which are harmful to personal relations." The notion of austerity is also to be found in Denis Goulet, who is quoted below (p. 73, note 15).

creates new needs . . . as a result, Gentlemen, it now happens—
can you believe my words?—as a result, I say, it now happens
that one can be poor yet lack nothing.''

Likewise, for La Bruyère, "the immediate occasion of poverty is
the neighbourhood of great wealth". Sismondi takes up the idea when
he says: "Wealth creates poverty.''

The Americans, we know, have adopted the well-known text
Desiderata, which dates from 1692 and was discovered in a Baltimore
church. It states simply:

"If you compare yourself with others you may become vain and
bitter, for always, there will be greater and lesser persons than
yourself."[9]

If the wisdom of this has not, too little known as it is, prevented the
flourishing of capitalism, the fact remains that *Desiderata* is close to
a refusal of ostentation as a model for development.

It may be remembered that in 1935 George Gershwin created
the characters of the American Negroes Porgy and Bess who, from the
depths of their poverty, declaimed and sang verses of wisdom that are
still popular:

"Oh! I got plenty o' nuttin
An' nuttin's plenty for me
I got no car, got no mule, *got no misery*."

If we leave the West for other regions, we know that the two great
Asian religions, Hinduism and Buddhism, hold that the ascetic life
enables the believer to attain transcendental purification.

Gandhi maintained that true civilization consisted not in multiplying
our needs but rather in restricting them voluntarily. This, he believed,
was the only way to find happiness and become more open to others.
To seek to create an infinitude of needs that would then have to be
satisfied was, in his view, an endless and useless quest.

---

[9] Quoted by Hazel Henderson: "The Decline of Jonesism", in *The Futurist*, October
1974. Inspired by this precept, Martin Luther King used to enjoy sharing with his
friends the well-known maxim of Douglas Mallock:
"If you cannot be a pine-tree on the hilltop, be a bush in the valley,
But be the best little bush on the bank of the brook . . .
If you cannot be the sun, be a star; it's not by size that you'll win;
Whatever you are, be the best."

Islam also has a great deal to say on the subject. There are the famous words of the prophet Mohammed: "O God, grant that I live poor and die poor." The Koran recounts the story of Karoon, an illustration of the paradox that fortune may be the enemy of the believer. Power through wealth may become a curse.

The word *dervish*, which is of Persian origin, means poor, and the dervishes are regarded as sages "who lift their eyes to pierce the celestial light, where all is truth".

Again, in Islam, we find the word *zakat* (equivalent to the *tzedakah* of the Hebrews), which means the offering of part of his fortune that the Moslem is expected to give for the poor. Abu Thar El Ghafair, however, thought that wealth should be divided among the whole population. He was against the existence of rich and poor in the same community. One of the best-known works in Arabic is the book of *Good and Evil*, which is in fact an anthology in praise of poverty. Another book, which appeared in the fifteenth century under the signature El Dalqi, as an illustration of *Poverty and the Poor*, is in fact a biography of scholars whose wisdom was all the greater, because of their poverty. This was the origin of the custom of signing a message "The poor and God-fearing so and so", which is practised in particular by the ulama, whose erudition and wisdom are well known.

The Arabs of today—and many others of the same faith—still follow the long trail first set forth in the Koran. Consider the men of Marrakech, Tizi Ouzou or Carthage. Though many of them recall their struggle—"I can love now only if consumed by rage"—they all seem to find long moments of happiness: "In the meaning of a glance, in the value of a quiet understanding", as Anna Gréki puts it.

And take the deep wisdom of the Negroes, wherever they may be found, Negroes of Benin, of Bahia, of Basse Terre, of Cuba, of Haiti or of Belize, whose proverbs, songs and dances speak of the poverty with which they are familiar and that means to each of them: "The plot of land made yours for the valour of your two arms, your fruit-trees all around, your cattle in the fields, all you need at hand and your freedom, whose only bounds are the seasons, good or bad, rain or drought" (Jacques Roumain).

Putting an end to exploitation and destitution

We must not be led astray by this religious and poetic idealizing of poverty. For the philosophy of an order based on God's will in which the rich and the poor should keep their place and the poor, in particular, should be satisfied with their lot—" . . . the poor shall never cease out of the land" (Deuteronomy)—has been widely used and exploited by many with the aim of dominating, subjugating and becoming wealthy by making others even more wretched.

People have even gone to the monstrous length of maintaining that the poor must exist always so that the rich may gain salvation through charity and alms.

In the *Sources*, Gratry denounces this spiritual justification of an unjust temporal order, saying that there is nothing Christian about the maxim that we must be miserable in this world in order to be happy in the next.[10]

The Industrial Revolution, which made possible the limitless creation of new goods through the application of science, energy and machines, also gave rise to the belief that limitless enrichment could come to all sooner or later. The belief in progress through wealth led to the illusion that moderation and a wholesome poverty were no longer valid as principles for living. Rising capitalism was unaware of the social contradictions it was creating. Pauperism appeared with the very beginning of industrial capitalism. The term *Verelendung*, as adopted by Karl Marx, refers precisely to the system that brings into existence a mass of people reduced to indigence and obliged to resort to public or private charity in order to survive.

Throughout Europe the extraordinarily wretched situation of the workers, their inhuman conditions of work and life and the extreme misery of the countryside aroused the indignation of thinkers and writers, including Léon Faucher, Robert Owen, Thomas Carlyle and Karl Biedermann.

Among them was also Charles Fourier, who rightly observes in *Le nouveau monde industriel et sociétaire*: "This vicious circle of industry has been so clearly recognized that on all sides people are

---

[10] The gospel according to Saint Mark, indeed, says that the man who gives up all shall receive a hundredfold even in this life (Mark x. 29, 30).

beginning to view it with suspicion and to be astonished that poverty should arise in a civilisation whose very foundation is plenty."

Napoleon III, the author of *L'extinction du paupérisme*, maintained that "poverty would no longer be seditious when wealth was no longer oppressive".

The turning point came with Marx and Engels. The destitute, on the fringe of industrial society, became the proletariat, and their potential strength was such that it was they, above all, who formed the revolutionary class, the class that would shortly destroy capitalism, seize power and build communism, proletarians who had nothing of their own to defend and must destroy all privileges.

The Manifesto of the Communist Party declares:

"Freeman and slave . . . , oppressor and oppressed, stood in constant opposition to one another, carried on an uninterrupted, now hidden, now open fight, a fight that each time ended either in a revolutionary reconstitution of society at large, or in the common ruin of the contending classes."

It became dangerous merely to be classed among the rich, the bourgeois and the powerful.

Marx was well aware of the risks of plenty: "The more the material world gains in value", he wrote, "the more the human world loses in value. One is directly related to the other." Again, writing to Ricardo: "They want production to be confined to useful things, but they forget that the production of too many useful things tends to make too many people useless." And finally, an idea that I find essential to the present subject and to the argument I am advancing here is that set forth among others by Marx in *Wage-Labour and Capitalism*:

"Whether a house be large or small, it meets all that is required of a dwelling from the social point of view as long as the surrounding houses are of the same size. If a palace is erected beside it, however, the little house shrivels up to become a hut . . . In vain it will stretch towards the sky with the advance of civilisation; its occupants will feel ever more uncomfortable, more dissatisfied, more cramped between their four walls, for it will always remain small if the neighbouring palace grows in the same, or greater proportions."

Rethinking the way to fulfilment

The broad survey that I have just presented, in the manner of a compendium, admittedly very incomplete, may serve, I hope, to justify my conception of poverty, which I look on as something useful, a lever in the machinery of development or a sheet-anchor in a world where one must constantly "rethink the way to fulfilment".

Poverty looked on in this way, not as a fatality calling for resignation, but as a positive value to be chosen freely, is a challenge to all the peoples of the world.

That is why I can consider the problem from the point of view both of the countries known as "developed" and, even more, of those generally referred to as the "Third World". I intend to base my argument on the reality experienced each day by men at work—and by men without work.

I set myself the task of determining how and why poverty, as redefined and redirected, constitutes without doubt the only avenue to independent development.

This approach is not due to any special taste for exalting moral virtues. It is due not to the romantic conception of the good poor or the noble savage, but rather to that of an inevitable and compelling utopia, in the sense that, as René Dumont said, the prospect for humanity today is "utopia or death".[11]

When I was discussing the plan of this book with Ivan Illich, we were in full agreement on one point that, in my view, is capital: the myth of the "golden age" has to be avoided. It is distasteful to hear well-fed people extolling the virtues of peoples that suffer from poverty. Poverty, when it destroys the flesh and the spirit, is no creator of positive values. Periods of want, famine and restrictions, though they call forth gestures of solidarity, also give rise to the worst forms of exploitation—black market, suddenly acquired rights and so on. On a more fundamental plane, poverty can affect the creative faculties, sometimes irreversibly. I have no desire to confuse adversity that degrades with adversity that ennobles.

This having been made clear, for it is the point on which Illich and

[11] See also Georg Picht: *Der Mut zur Utopie* (Munich, R. Piper, 1969). A French translation was published under the title *Réflexions au bord du gouffre* (Paris, Laffont, 1974).

I were in profound agreement, we also agreed about extravagant appeals intended to arouse feelings about poverty, propaganda that tries to dramatize destitution and displays masses of people in rags— the indelicate showing of hunger-drawn faces on cinema and television screens and in specialized journals—all that,we felt, was morbid.

It is not from such a vision of poverty, I maintain, that a positive model can be derived for development.

The psychological impulses aroused by such campaigns seem to me to be highly suspect. The purpose is to establish affluence as an aim, as a mode of life. Wealth then becomes the model and synonym of development.

In Upper Volta, where, despite the harshness of reality, a rare and courageous policy of democratic dialogue still finds expression, observers noted some time ago a reaction among young professional workers against what they called "miserabilism". For example, the following remarks by a young teacher appeared in the report of a special committee on the national economy set up in April 1976:

"Among the nations of the world Upper Volta is the last or the last but one of the twenty-five poorest countries. This situation has been aggravated by the recent drought, which was at its worst in 1973. Our destitution is paraded at every level. Even our governors in their official speeches contrive to proclaim our poverty, so successfully, indeed, that one journalist has suggested that Upper Volta should simply be removed from the map of the world since it was not viable."

Such attitudes are not uncommon in countries where there is not enough food to go round. We are all familiar with the technique of exhibiting sores to arouse pity, in Bangladesh and other countries.

It is well known, however, that charity neither solves problems nor rectifies structural defects. Nor is this all; for history shows that it leads to dangerous compromises, from which even the most venerable institutions, with the Church at their head, have not been immune.

Unrestrained accumulation and the social control of needs

Books on development are appearing every day to show that what matters is not to have but to be, and in this connection an inhabitant

of Upper Volta could doubtless provide a lesson for many. To break
the snare of mass consumption is no longer empty talk: it has become
a necessity, a necessity that will lead, as we shall see further on, to a
development strategy based on "the social control of needs"; for otherwise "basic needs" become unlimited and thus, through the too familiar process of "self-perpetuating frustration", are never satisfied. [12]

To view existence and to plan development through the unending
spiral of acquiring goods of questionable worth, which are not essential
and require obsessive and perpetual pursuit—this is the height of
absurdity. It is also a rear-guard action for the peoples of the Third
World, at the very time when many voices in the West are already
calling for a truer appreciation of human welfare, based not only on
level of living, but also, and indeed more, on better conditions of life
and on a life of real quality.

As we have all learnt in our school books, the simplest definition
of man is that he is a reasonable animal. If, therefore, we do not
want to take him only as a "fattened pig", neither of these two
ontological elements of the human being must be apprehended without
the other. Development then becomes that which favours the satisfaction
of all our basic needs, including those of the reason and so of the
spirit. If this view of material and spiritual balance is adopted in

---

[12] It is interesting in this connection to refer to Schopenhauer's analysis of "will" (in
the sense of desires and appetites). The following extracts are offered for consideration:

"Every desire arises from a need, and so from privation and so from distress.
Satisfied, the need vanishes; but, for one desire satisfied, at least ten remain unappeased.
No desire can lead to lasting and stable satisfaction. That which is received is always
alms cast at the feet of a beggar, alms that prolongs his life today in order to prolong
his suffering tomorrow. Thus we obtain neither rest nor lasting happiness so long as
we give ourselves over to the urge of our desires . . . Without rest no well-being is
possible. The man dominated by desire is attached to the revolving wheel of Ixion;
he is ever filling the sieve of the Danaides; he is Tantalus burning with everlasting
thirst.

"But when an outside circumstance or inner harmony snatches us suddenly from the
unending torrent of will, tears our consciousness away from enslavement to our
desires, our attention contemplates things in freedom, as representations and not as
impulses. When this happens, the calm that is ever sought after but ever fugitive
appears spontaneously. We feel that all is well. It is the painless state extolled by
Epicurus as the supreme good, as the state of the gods. At that moment we are set
free from the heavy urge of will; we observe the sabbath in the forced labour imposed
on us by desire; the wheel of Ixion stops . . . What does it matter then whether we see
the sunset through the window of a palace or through the bars of a dungeon?"

defining the degree of development and the criterion of mental health is added, I agree with Johan Galtung that the evaluation of a country that is called developed, while 30 per cent of its sick are in psychiatric hospitals, must be reconsidered.

Absurd, indeed, is the unrestrained accumulation that ends by becoming a poison in the body of society.

It is true that the biological analogy applied to social realities often leads to false interpretations,[13] but it does make striking comparisons possible. I can thus point out that biology teaches that there is accumulation when a substance is introduced into a body and not eliminated. The substance is, or becomes, toxic. If ontogenesis reduces phylogenesis and is explained by it, wealth, when it means the uncontrolled accumulation of private property, in the long run becomes toxic for society, just as fat is generally toxic for the body. The affluent society, in fact, if unchecked and uncontrolled, becomes sick from the wealth it has created by inflating its reserves of superfluous goods.

The wealth of the industrial societies in reality hides increasing distress.

There are many books to make it clear that, if Western industrial societies have inexhaustible supplies of cosmetics, fancy plastic goods and elegant cars, the ecological, social and human costs to which these also give rise defy our understanding, whether we consider polluted air and water, the decay of towns and urban congestion, the breaking down of social structures, drug addiction or violence.[14]

The creators of industrial societies refused to see anything but the fantastic inventive powers released by scientific and technical progress. It has taken too long to realize the equally fantastic powers of destruction inherent in industrial processes.

François Ramade[15] describes many cases where man acts as a predator

---

[13] See Pierre Achard, Antoinette Chauvenet *et al.*: *Discours biologique et ordre social* (Paris, Editions du Seuil, 1977).

[14] For a detailed analysis and a theoretical explanation of these manifestations reference may be made to J. Galbraith: *The Affluent Society* (Harmondsworth, Penguin Books, 1962); Vance Packard: *The Status Seekers* (New York, McKay, 1959); A. Toffler: *Future Shock* (New York, Random House, 1970); J. P. Dupuy and Jean Robert: *La trahison de l'opulence* (Paris, Presses universitaires de France, 1976).

[15] François Ramade: *Eléments d'écologie appliquée* (Paris, Ediscience, 1974).

Dethroning Money

as though he did not himself belong to the ecosystem whose equilibrium he is destroying.

Georgescu-Roegen[16] has shown that every system of production is really a system producing waste. Waste appears at every stage in the processing of a raw material—from extraction to the use of the product, which itself ends by being thrown away or destroyed.

The more production expands, the more pollution increases. The more sophisticated the production, the more dangerous the pollution. The pollution of seas and rivers by chemicals affects even the regions which are farthest away from the industrial complexes where it originates.

It is well known that spent electric batteries, which are regularly thrown away on rubbish dumps not far from rivers, contain a high proportion of mercury.

Months after escaping from the Seveso works, of tragic renown, dioxin continues to claim new victims. And no day passes without a new Seveso on a smaller scale. The anxiety provoked by the falling on Canadian territory of the nuclear satellite Cosmos 954 will not be soon forgotten.

When the air is "over" polluted at Los Angeles, observes René Dumont, the inhabitants are advised *"not to breathe"*. Will the whole planet soon have to *"stop breathing"*?

Rabelais and Montaigne denounced "science without conscience".

When man breathes polluted air, lives in the midst of noise, eats food treated with preserving and colouring agents, works in an undertaking whose mechanism he ignores or does not understand, when he passes a good part of his time in crammed transport and returns each evening to the niche allotted him in a dormitory town, I cannot agree that he is rich, I cannot agree that he is developed.

In his book *The Harried Leisure Class*, the Swedish economist Stafan Linden sets out to show that, as affluence increases, time becomes scarcer, for consumption takes time. To buy, use and maintain private cars, boats, swimming-pools and sports equipment much time is needed, first to earn the necessary money and then to enjoy it. This is confirmed by Walter Weisskopf when he points out that the

[16] N. Georgescu-Roegen, *The Entropy Law and the Economic Process* (Cambridge, Mass., Harvard University Press, 1971).

true dimensions of poverty are existential rather than economic. Jacques Attali sums up well what I feel: society has become reduced to "the collective organisation of the individual's destruction of time".[17]

Is this existence, which has nothing to do with true life, really what we want? To waste time or to take one's time: this brings to mind the Bedouin to whom progress was being explained. With a recently constructed railway line, he was told, he could cross the desert in 4 hours, whereas previously it would have taken him a week.

"Good," said the Bedouin, "but how should I spend the rest of the time?" The question is worth pondering on.

Time, our first form of wealth if we wish to possess the world, to see it, to know it, to come to terms with it, cannot be reduced to money.

The race for money, ever more money, cannot provide this wealth of time, and we come to the absurd situation where the more the wealth of a nation seems to increase, the more, in fact, its human destitution becomes clear; for the quality of life of every person and of the whole community tends to diminish. It is no longer entirely surprising, for example, to hear Philippe de Weck, Chairman of the Union Bank of Switzerland, insist on "the social responsibility of the banks in a free economy".[18] But let us concentrate briefly on another and equally significant source of concern.

The ills of industrial civilization

There is no better indicator of people's well-being than their personal health. If it cannot be denied that medicine has made real advances, neither is there any doubt that the problems of health are far from being solved. What are known as the diseases of civilization—various forms of cancer, cardio-vascular troubles, nervous breakdowns—are becoming commoner and affecting ever younger people, to an extent that sometimes seems to reach epidemic proportions—and this is happening in almost every industrialized country.

The pharmaceutical industry has never been so prosperous. A per-

[17] Jacques Attali: *La parole et l'outil* (Paris, Presses universitaires de France, 1976).

[18] Public lecture given at the IILS in February 1977.

fectly innocent book giving the composition and use of medicines has created an uproar among the pharmaceutical chemists of a certain European country, because the author maintains that most of the products are replaceable and of little use. The scientism of the medical establishment acts as much on the minds of the sick as on their bodies. A survey has shown that, of 100 persons cured by taking medicines, 70 had, without their knowledge, been taking placebos. These substances, devoid of all curative value, had nevertheless been remarkably effective. This is another example of waste and fraud, as is rightly pointed out by Orio Giarini, with whom I have begun a study of the matter as part of the work of the International Institute for Labour Studies.

The ills of industrial civilization stem from two basic principles that underlie increased production and profit: concentration and specialization. The first means the concentration of man in towns, of production in large units, of power in few hands.

Specialization means the splitting up of tasks for the worker and the proliferation of specialists at every level. The witch-doctors of today are those who have knowledge, the engineers and technocrats with their hermetic and inaccessible jargon. Through concentration and specialization the structures of society are changing, sometimes dangerously.[19]

In contrast with the growing frustration of industrial societies we can turn to the profound wealth of many societies in Africa and Asia, where the family brings together under one roof the direct and collateral relations of several generations. The insane live in the village, are accepted and feel that they are acknowledged. As soon as industrialization turns people into specialists, however, every change from a closed-circuit economy to an exchange economy is accompanied by a reduction of the family to its simplest form.

The accumulative society has a remarkable power of recuperation. There are growing numbers of hospitals, rest homes, special schools

---

[19] This is what Michel Bosquet has in mind when he observes:
". . . Technique is not neutral: it reflects and determines the relation of the producer to the product, the worker to his work, the individual to the group and society, man to his environment; it is the shaper of power relations, social production relations and the hierarchical division of tasks." *Ecologie et liberté* (Paris, Editions Galilée, 1977).

and holiday camps where different classes of specialists in social rehabilitation practise their art (every kind of recreation officer, social worker and educator). But does the society itself really exist? We may well ask, indeed, whether the society is not accumulating a debt of social and ecological costs rather than riches. And it is not hard to see that the throwaway economy seems to be at the end of its tether. Especially as internal costs, even production costs, are increasing constantly and a phase of diminishing returns from technology is being reached. The possibilities of inventing new products based on a given technique are being exhausted.

As the chain between basic research and the utilization of the product lengthens and becomes more complex, so the new technologies call for more multidisciplinary capacity. The more the costs of research grow, the more, inevitably, the time needed for the new developments increases, even when industry and the public have meanwhile made enormous progress in the ability to glimpse the use of a new research finding. Experts are wondering whether, in several sectors, we have not come to the point of having exploited the bulk of the opportunities opened by the impact of science on technology since the end of the last century.[20]

In the field of big computers, for example, IBM announced in March 1975 that it was cutting down the programme of innovations for 1976.

There are more and more technological bottle-necks, for example, in the manufacture of synthetic fibres. In this field all the possibilities of transforming basic molecules seem to have been explored. The unwoven fibres have not turned out to be of the quality, nor have they had the success, that was expected and this has been a clear loss to the economy.

In certain sectors, moreover, the complexity of production is such that the constant diversification that is necessary if production is to be competitive has become unprofitable and impossible. And so the durability of the products is reduced. A motor-car or a refrigerator is designed to last 5 years. Raw materials are thus wasted in the

[20] Orio Giarini: *Introduction à l'économie du risque et de la sécurité*, Unpublished paper, March 1976, p. 33.

manufacture of "gadgets". Under different wrapping-papers the wood of our forests is used to envelop identical products.

This loss of our heritage and the destruction of our traditional values disclose the great vulnerability of the economic system. "Grow rich" proposed Guizot when the immense expansion of industry was beginning. Today we wonder for whom and why we should grow rich. Rich in possessions often means poor in understanding.

The questioning begins

Among the millions of docile consumers, however, the voices of discontent are growing louder and louder.

During the 1960s in the United States and elsewhere, it was the war in Viet-Nam that was first called into question; many young men deserted, demanding peace and justice and, at the same time, an end to racialism and sexual discrimination.

Small autonomous communities began to come into existence. But the situation has evolved since then. It is reported, for example, that a professor of the Energy Center of the University of Florida, Howard Todum, has won fame by declaring that the Organisation of Petroleum Exporting Countries deserved the Nobel Prize in 1973, for it had done more than all the schools, all the universities and all the leaders to make the inhabitants of the United States, Western Europe and Japan realize that they had to abandon an economy of waste. It was certainly a shock for the world to find itself facing the spectre of want, which it had forgotten about since the end of the Second World War. Were the predictions of the Club of Rome right? "Halt growth", "utopia or death", "the poisoned banquet"—these were so many cries of alarm that continued to trouble people's minds. There was lively discussion everywhere. Groups of citizens were formed in America, Japan, Europe and Australia who set about exposing the diseconomies, constraints and inconveniences carefully ignored by the economists as mere "extraneous factors" of production. The time has passed when the opponents of nuclear energy were long-haired hippies; today they are businessmen, teachers and women who have their children's future in mind. Such pressure groups have managed, in California for example, to have plans for the building of motorways abandoned and the credits allocated to the expansion of public transport and the production of energy from non-polluting sources. It is now not only a few "starry-eyed ecologists" who demand a better quality of life: more and more people are raising questions and dissatisfaction is spreading to ever wider strata of the population. The ordinary American no longer considers his way of life to be the best in the world. A survey made public in 1976, which was based on 1497 adults representative of American opinion,[21] bears witness to a profoundly changed attitude of public opinion in the United States. The public understands that pollution and waste are related and are "very serious" for the country.

First of all, an inversion of priorities is taking place in respect of personal property and social services. Whereas 42 per cent of the persons questioned considered it essential to arouse in the consumer the desire to buy new products, 61 per cent attached great importance to the institution of better and more modern social services.

Furthermore, over 74 per cent realized that, because of their high level of consumption, raw materials and products were becoming scarcer and dearer, recognizing the relation between the quantity of products consumed and constant inflation.

This shows a significant attitude, since 61.2 per cent of Americans consider it morally wrong for their country, which contains 6 per cent of the inhabitants of the globe, to consume 40 per cent of the energy and raw materials produced.

For 55.3 per cent of the persons questioned this disparity between population and consumption is prejudicial to the welfare of the rest of the world, and 50.3 per cent think that the rest of the world will turn against the Americans if natural resources remain so unevenly distributed.

Over 90 per cent, or almost all those questioned, envisage the need for a change of attitude. We must, they say, find here in our own country the means of putting an end to the accumulation of things that we consume and throw away. Still more surprising is the fact that they feel the need for a controlled reduction in their level of living.

[21] *The Harris Survey*, December 1975.

Thus, 77.8 per cent of those questioned are in favour of a very different way of life, where people would no longer feed animals with beef and renew their wardrobe every year to keep in style and where cars would be kept till they had done 100,000 miles. To reduce the cost of housing, 66.3 per cent would even be willing for people to have fewer weekend cottages and to live in blocks of flats rather than private houses.

The armaments race—and no thought of death!

There is now a far more telling field of challenge where, although results are limited so far, the future is full of promise: denunciation of the armaments race.

This leads to a reference that is essential to our analysis. Raymond Aron, in his own way, makes it perfectly clear in his book *Paix et guerre entre les nations* when he writes:

"The poverty in every society known since the dawn of civilisation, the uneven distribution of wealth within and among communities, the immensity of the wealth which may be obtained by violence compared with that obtainable by work, all these facts have constituted unremittingly the fundamental condition governing conflicts between classes or between states; because of them wars of conquest seem in retrospect to have been rational."

Wealthy societies are thus forced to assume the form of strongly organized police states. They suffer the same lot as societies that worship power and fear to lose it. If accumulation is restricted and power is not made a principal object, this automatically limits the inevitably futile struggles, carried out under cover or openly, which stem from an obstinate feeling of insecurity on one side and boundless frustration on the other.

Porgy again has something to tell us:

"De folks wid plenty o' plenty
Got to pray all de day.
Seems wid plenty you sure got to worry
How to keep de debble away . . ."

The model of the advanced industrial society, despite the criticisms of some of its members, leads to situations of incalculable tragedy.

The armaments race is the direct appendage of the society where wealth and power are not shared. Countries arm and fight at home and abroad against the envy of those who call for a different distribution of property, against those who call for greater equality, fuller participation and more freedom.

If we turn against the wealth that ends in annihilation we discover poverty, the poverty that leads us back to the true life and so, since this is in the nature of things, helps us to accept death as human beings: *Fugit irreparabile tempus*, as Virgil put it long ago.

Indeed, it is always in a graveyard, by a tomb, that the word "vanity" takes on a meaning and the word "poverty" stands out with all its force. Festugière reminds us of this in the most striking way:

"One after the other the generations are born, eat, drink, mate, reproduce, raise themselves a little, make perhaps a certain stir, fall asunder, then die—and all has been said . . . The day will come when this mould that we form on the surface of the earth will even have ceased to be a dream . . . Of all the history of men, of our loves and hates, of our pathetic desires to last, of all we have suffered for good, of the patience of the old, of the tears of the child in the night, nothing will remain, nothing . . . One more move, and then of you, of me nothing will remain."[22]

I add, to round off my argument, "nothing will remain . . . *here*".

Wisdom of this sort, however, does not linger in the mind. That is the way we are made: something moves us for a moment and then vanishes like a dream as soon as the animal in us regains the upper hand. "No longer a fire in the depths of my heart . . ."

We are held captive by Mercury, the God of traffickers, by Mammon and by all the devils of all the ages, defenceless and almost unthinking. Under their sway we are fascinated by money, power and pleasure. The very idea of death sometimes becomes a stimulant to possess more.

I am not attacking lavish expenditure on funerals or burial ceremonies. After all, as they say in the land of the Yorubas, if we have not chosen to respect the living, we can at least pay honour to the dead.

It is much more disturbing to hear a young heiress, in a great hurry,

---

[22] *L'enfant d'Agrigente* (Paris, Editions du Cerf, 1950).

47307

tense, sick for money, let out the cry: "It's the sale of Mother's property that I'm concerned about."

The real problem lies there. And it is to be found wherever death is not the source of solidarity, making the dead person a link in the family structure.[23]

When Alex Haley, searching for his African "roots" as an American black, decided to bring to life the Gambia of his ancestors, he too turned to death as an agent of solidarity. The scene describing the end of Yaissa, little Kunta's grandmother, is worth mentioning, in particular the lesson drawn from it by Omoro, the father of the weeping lad:

" . . . For many days", writes Haley, "Kunta hardly ate or slept, and he would not go anywhere with his Kafo[24] mates. So grieved was he that Omoro, one evening, took him to his own hut, and there beside his bed, speaking to his son more softly and gently than he ever had before, told him something that helped to ease his grief. He said that three groups of people lived in every village. First were those you could see—walking around, eating, sleeping and working. Second were the ancestors whom Grandma Yaissa had now joined.

"And the third people—who are they?" asked Kunta.

"The third people", said Omoro, "are those waiting to be born."

Haley's passionate search for his ancestry can be understood by anyone who compares this solidarity between generations with the grasping and lonely society in which so many black Americans say that they live today.

On her return from America, Myriam Makeba devoted a satirical song to a widow who went on dancing in her lover's arms when her unfortunate husband's death was announced and came out of her trance only when she heard that his will was going to be made public.

---

[23] A source of solidarity, for the dead person continues to be active and to communicate his "virtue" to his descendants and remains an example for the living that it is their duty to carry on.

[24] Kafo: group of children of the same age.

Listening and observing

The reader may be surprised at the importance I attach here to the popular song. I believe that, like the written word, song often expresses, through images, longing or fulfilment, the distress of solitude or the joy of living communities. I share the view of Jacques Attali when he writes:

". . . the world is not looked at, it is heard. It is not read, it is listened to. . . . Nothing important happens without sound. . . . We must learn, then, to judge a society by its sounds, by its art and by its amusements rather than by its statistics."[25]

In ancient times, the theatre gave a special place to the chorus, which enabled the people to take part in what was going on. Long ago a song of Rhodes, "The Swallow", invited Greeks and Romans to rid themselves of all that was not essential.

Today, youth can still offer us the freshness we need. Apart from sentimental clichés or escapist dreams, the records our children bring back from school may also strike some true notes.

Serge Lama, for example, points to the paradox of the frustrated rich, who seek safety in "our attics devoid of lifts".

And there is the persuasive Guy Béart making us realize that everything moves, changes, has already changed, since "bourgeois children play at poverty, at a hard life, at the Commune, at revolt" and that sometimes "these children, playing with words, will break a few links in our chains". Everything changes; for "children are heralds, each with a vital spark, proclaiming that the whole earth is the Messiah".

The whole earth . . .

The memory of a journey to China haunts me still.

The visitor to Peking does not pass through a poverty-stricken or wretched city. Peking no doubt displays a certain austerity. The people do not go about in motor-cars (the idea of the private car has no equivalent in Chinese) but life there does not seem to be unpleasant. The impression, I think, is the same as that formed by François Perroux when he visited Moscow a good many years ago. In Peking, too, an observer might conclude from the outward appearance of the

---

[25] Jacques Attali: *Bruits* (Paris, Presses universitaires de France, 1977), p. 7.

city that it resembles a Christian society where the essential articles of faith and ethics are, at last, being taken seriously.

"Our Church" writes Perroux "has never recommended private luxury or a super abundance of unnecessary goods or a nicely shaded diversification of consumer goods when the basic needs of the masses are not met."

I do not, however, claim that China provides a model. China has its own problems, which it solves in its own way and, having read the book of Broyelle and Tschirhart,[26] I cannot help having some doubts. . .

Nevertheless, in my view, Chinese society of today, even with the changes wrought by the pragmatism of Teng Tsiao Ping, still seems to be putting into practice the kind of poverty which I have defined here. So we find ourselves back again at the cross-roads of the same sources, the "Sources" of Alphonse Gratry, in which I read that "Poverty is neither destitution nor indigence. It is everyday life won by labour. It is something sacred, to be respected, to be prized, to be sought after."

A change of course

Poverty, as it can be observed in China, is beginning to emerge as an aim in the thought of Western societies. For example, Enrico Berlinguer has declared:

"Today, austerity is not a mere tool of cyclical policy designed to overcome passing economic difficulties and lead to recovery and the re-establishment of the old economic and social machinery . . . For us austerity is a means of dealing at the roots with a system that has entered into a structural crisis and of laying the foundations of a new system."

From every side, then, unrestrained wealth is being called into question as are the privileges derived from it. Everything proclaims the right of all to share goods and property. Why should the Third World adopt a model that has broken down and has sometimes even

---

[26] Claudie and Jacques Broyelle and Evelyne Tschirhart: *Deuxième retour de Chine* (Paris, Editions du Seuil, 1977).

turned out to be positively harmful? After all, development is surely an effort to conquer oneself and work with others, an effort that relies on the natural environment to meet the basic needs of the family and—through solidarity—of the group.

This conception of development has no need of a model. Yet this is not the path we are taking.

Turning our back on our history and geography, our arts and our skill, we reject growth based on our own strength and resources. Putting the immediate interests of the few before the long term benefit of all, we prefer to widen the narrow circle of the privileged from time to time and to go on stifling the energy of the great majority of the people.

It is no credit to us, as Sembène Ousmane points out, that thousands of people do not even own a filtering jar for drinking water, while some use mineral water, imported from Europe, to fill the radiator of their cars with the dubious intention of keeping it from clogging.

Money, whose slaves we have become, dictates all our extravagances, all our failings, all our excesses.

Because of the money that we must have *at all costs*, we are in danger of finding ourselves with no more true culture, no freedom, no respect for anything, no family.

Verres and Catiline arise on all sides, but there is no Cicero to denounce the growing mass of scandals. Here and there, on every continent, as someone from Amnesty International has put it, Nero takes over, more arrogant than ever. Then the time of martyrs has arrived. Henceforward, only they can accomplish the miracle.

You say I am too pessimistic? That such statements are totally groundless? This would be true were I unable to provide proof of our folly.

Alas, we go on walking on our hands—it is perfectly obvious. Bairoch has written: *Le tiers monde dans l'impasse* (The Third World at a Dead End). Before him, Dumont had written: *False Start in Africa.*

We always turned a deaf ear.

How long will this go on?

CHAPTER II

Upside Down
or The Folly of Mimicry

"Fari, he-haw! Fari, he-haw!
Fari is a donkey . . .
But where is Fari, the queen
  of the donkeys,
Who went off . . . and has
  not returned?"
    Popular song quoted in
Les contes d'Amadou Koumba
        (Birago Diop)

"It is high time to bring those
negroes to their senses who
believe that revolution consists
in throwing out the white man
and taking over, by which I
mean playing at being whites
at the expense of the blacks."
        (Aimé Césaire.
La tragédie du Roi Christophe)

Everyone who undertakes official missions on behalf of some
government or international organization knows how warmly he is
welcomed in most of the developing countries which he visits.
Naturally I share this feeling. I am nevertheless extremely embarrassed
when the warmth of such a welcome smacks of ostentation and
snobbery unsuitable to the occasion. Thus in a certain tropical country
it has become a common custom not only among "well off" people
but even among those of more modest means for visitors to be offered
cool champagne "specially flown in from Europe",[1] whereas they
would have been perfectly satisfied with a cup of tea or coffee or
a glass of orange or pineapple juice.

---

[1] This practice led to such abuses that the Government of Nigeria, for example,
recently issued a decree prohibiting the import of champagne. But this does not seem to
have disturbed the habits of some people who are clever enough to "make out".

26

The pitfall of "good" manners . . .

This anecdote shows how dependency, if prolonged, can give rise to perverse reactions.

The ways of the man on top become the accepted standards: if he has succeeded in getting there it is because there is something special about him which sets him above other men and makes them follow him.

Even if I am not reconciled to my dependent status, I am inclined to recognize that power and to wish to wield it one day myself with all its advantages.

This is the trap we have fallen into. We have become *impressed* by our rulers. The ease with which they went about everything finally captivated us . . . Furthermore, in certain instances independence was formally proclaimed by the "transfer of powers".

"Transfer of powers", or more precisely the transfer of the forms of power, suggests a "transfer" of attitudes and conduct. Mimicry was thus extended to cover structures and patterns of political and social organization.

Sure of ourselves, naive, by pure logic we obeyed a faultless syllogism. More correctly expressed, we allowed ourselves to be caught up in the machinery of a polysyllogism as inflexible as fate. This could be stated as follows:

> "All independent countries throughout the world have a President at their head, who heads a government made up of some 20-30 ministries. They all have embassies abroad and a seat at the UN, and are kept in power by a tough police force and an army equipped with tanks and 'Mirages'. Every one of them sets up a national university and a national airline. They all proclaim their sovereignty by means of a national flag and a national anthem."

Now the Democratic Republic of Kilimandjaro has just been proclaimed a sovereign and independent State.

Therefore the Democratic Republic of Kilimandjaro has to have a flag, an army, a university, etc.

I go further.

Every political leader of all independent countries throughout the world lives in a well-guarded palace, drives around in a black limousine escorted by motor-cycle outriders, possesses secret funds, numerous secondary residences around the world, etc..

Now, the political rulers of Kilimandjaro have just been chosen by popular vote.

Therefore the political rulers of Kilimandjaro must drive around in black limousines escorted by motor-cycle outriders, etc. . . .

If we follow on with this argument, we find that:

All the ambassadors, all the members of all the parliaments, the generals, directors general, religious leaders, ideologists, all the first ladies of all the independent countries, are, say, do . . .

Now, Kilimandjaro . . .

Therefore Kilimandjaro . . .

Enough of our little game. Of course I was being facetious, but not all that much, and the reader will have seen that my intention was to point up a truism: we are wallowing in a sophism which misleads us, so profound and far-reaching are its repercussions.

Anyone who has read *The Lion and the Pearl* by Wole Soyinka, the Nigerian playwright, will doubtless recall the young teacher, Lakounlé, an authentic example of such mimicry, who promises his fiancée Sidi: "I shall teach you how to waltz, we shall learn the fox-trot together and spend our weekends in the night-clubs of Ibadan."

This is exactly the kind of thing that Labiche condemned in his *La poudre aux yeux* where he teaches us a lesson which is still valid today:

"To create a sensation, we must have style and show off! It's the fashion today. We try to dazzle each other. We swagger around. We blow ourselves up like balloons. And when we are all puffed up with vanity, rather than admit it, rather than say 'we are just two decent simple people', we prefer to throw away our future and our children's happiness."[2]

Throwing away the future . . . here we are at the heart of the problem.

It is not right to say or suggest that the rulers of national communities in the Third World are not seeking effectiveness in their development

---

[2] Act II, scene 13.

programmes. On the contrary, they all want development. They want it all the more keenly since they hope it will remain after them as a meaningful achievement justifying their effort.

Freud pinpointed narcissism as a prime factor of human behaviour: its many ways of expressing itself in forms of ostentation are a means of highlighting the existence and the importance of an individual.

By promoting a type of "development" which is conceived in the form of the most colossal budget, the most advanced technology, the most dazzling capital city, the aim is to justify national narcissism. There is no denial of other dimensions of development. But rather there is an inclination to ignore priorities.

A brief analysis of the consequences of that kind of attitude could be applied to such fields as culture and education, rural economy, industry and urbanization. It will reveal that such attitudes merely reinforce dependence, do nothing to honour reason and lead us to the impasse of what I call "counter-development".[3]

Culture, the epiphenomenon of development?

In 1958, along with Sembène Ousmane and several others, I represented the African Society for Culture at the first Conference of Afro-Asian Writers, held in Tashkent, Soviet Uzbekistan. We were trying to lay the foundations of an autonomous cultural life for our peoples.

Later, as Minister of Information in my country's first months of independence, I witnessed reality in action, and I can testify that when a country becomes independent attention to culture is side-tracked to "a later date". So many things are urgent. The matters of moment are political, economic and social. They also become self-assertive thanks to a cunning and well-oiled tacit understanding. While enjoying the illusion of being master in our own house, we are expected to produce and sell in the modern world to which we feel we ought to belong and where we hope to play a part. That means

---

[3] In my opinion, counter-development exists when a country has the means, however modest, of taking care of the basic needs of its people but diverts them to further non-priority, antisocial objectives, thereby enhancing the privileges of the minority.

Upside Down

becoming accepted in that world, behaving as is required by its standards.

It is for instance almost 20 years since most of Africa's independent countries first appeared on the international stage. Dare I say it? The problem of their cultural identity is still virtually unchanged. Very occasionally some tribute is paid to "authenticity" and freedom from constraint, but the mentality of the colonized is still firmly there.

The reason for this is that mercantile capitalism has trapped us in a vicious circle which we have not yet been able to break. And if we want to keep up a minimum of exchange with it, the terms of the dialogue have to obey the accepted rules.

Here the notion of exchange value as opposed to use value takes on its full meaning. Mercantile exchange entails the alienation of one of the partners to the other, and exchange value kills use value.

Normally, use value would enhance the importance of the languages of Africa, which are effectively used in everyday life and which give expression to concerns, wisdom, feelings.[4]

But exchange value prevails, since the extraverted economy demands the maintenance of links with the "Mother country", with the "Centre" as Samir Amin puts it. The monetary system, the system of measures, production circuits and patterns of consumption all dance to the tune of exchange value which holds them in its grip. As everyone knows, it is an unfair exchange. But there is less awareness of the influence which all this exerts on the people's authentic culture. If Europe is being Americanized, it shows up first in the language. Words like "snack", "self-service", "drugstore", "tee-shirt" or "hit parade" are not merely neologisms. They indicate a cultural influence and a powerful presence in everyday life.

To use J. Berque's expression, language is the "home of the being", a basic factor, a vital foundation on which to base any policy for national construction. If it is true that foreign languages undoubtedly open the doors to the great treasures of culture, as soon as they cease to be "foreign" and become national languages they provide others,

---

[4] See article by Yves Person in *Jeune Afrique*, No. 853 of 13 May 1977.

as Joseph Ki-Zerbo remarks, with "the key to the treasures of our minds".[5] They then become a vehicle of domination, the best possible travelling salesmen, turning us into buyers of all manner of products which foreigners send us together with instructions which we can now read.

In the Western context, the strength of Japan lies in its profound and, in my opinion, quasi-permanent resistance to any lasting cultural assimilation. A short stay in Tokyo soon shows us that, notwithstanding its sky-scrapers and American-type hotels, Japanese culture represents a use value for everyone, constituting an essential element in the terms of exchange. Everybody is not only obliged to buy "Japanese", but if they want to do business they must accept the fact that the national culture examines and corrects inventions and products and the way in which they are offered to the Japanese public. Exchange is only possible on that basis.

Capitalism in Japan is probably as all-consuming as elsewhere. It is even reasonable to fear that the Japanese individual is the victim of a permanent ambivalence between his productive life and his sociocultural life. My purpose here, however, was merely to show how the Japanese managed to marry their authentic culture with their economic vitality.

The road which most of us are following leads to a cultural impasse, with no assurance of economic development. To quote Joseph Ki-Zerbo once more, "When in countries which are 80 or 90% illiterate the administration relies solely on the written word, on paper as country folk call it, on identity cards, tax receipts, etc., and the law limits the vote to those who can read and write in French", the alien language becomes "a tool of production used for the privileged development of a minority, mandarin-like class".

There would seem to have been little change since the days of the colonial decree: "Teaching must be in French. The use of local dialects is forbidden in all schools, both private and public." Bernard Dadié's novel *Climbie* tells how, as a young pupil in the alien school, he

---

[5] *Culture et développement*, public lecture, International Institute for Labour Studies, Geneva, November 1976.

reacted against the rule prohibiting the use of his mother tongue even for talking with other children: anyone disobeying the rule was punished and made to sweep and clean the school.

Admittedly, the notorious "Our ancestors the Gauls" has finally been dropped from the panoply of easy criticism, having vanished from our history books. But here and there, in the law-courts, judges still dispense justice with the assistance of interpreters as they did during colonial times. And we have to admit that the situation is pretty hopeless in a number of countries which have no indigenous written language and no general, scientific or technical literature. The main thing, they say, is to practise exchange with others—immediately—by means of languages *at present* available. There appears to be no answer to this. Yet it should be possible to try to enrich and transcribe the indigenous languages and to make this effort a part of an over-all policy of indigenous development, which could help show the way to progress while respecting local cultural identity.

That is why I remain convinced that accepting the uncontrolled use of foreign languages because of our colonial past has led us to commit cultural murder which facilitates our permanent subjection to an alienating economic pattern.

We are truly in the position described by Sylvain Bemba in *Tarentelle noire et diable blanc (Black Tarantella and White Devil)*, where he shows young blacks selling their souls to the white devil, Faustino, in order to be allowed to climb the greasy pole festooned with manufactured goods. No one succeeds in reaching the top and they all end up exhausted.

Transfer or exchange?

This pattern of thought and conduct explains why today we talk of "transfer of technology" and "international division of labour".

In his *Réforme intellectuelle et morale (Intellectual and Moral Reform)* Renan had already put forward a dismal international division of labour:

"Chinese in the factory, Arabs and Negroes in the fields, with the 'others' to carry on with the noble skills of the cape and the sword.''[6]

This makes it easier to understand why there are jobs in certain countries, in Europe for instance, which any unemployed person will turn down in advance and which must automatically be given to immigrant workers.

We appear to have accepted as a kind of destiny that we should be cast in certain roles in life, predetermined by those more powerful than ourselves while our cultures are relegated to the marginal status of folklore. We have thus helped to legitimize a division of labour which denies us the right to a specific share in the global development of an interdependent world through a clearly determined regional autonomy. If we "regionalized" culture, if we broadened the use of Swahili and Yoruba and gave more importance to Bambara, would we not encourage the development of stimulating cross-bred cultures which would in no way obviate the use of foreign languages for specific purposes and a general extension of knowledge?

As to "transfer of technology", it presupposes displacement without compensation, and constitutes in my view a profoundly ambiguous notion. Far be it from me to deny the value of those transfers of technology which have been successfully effected throughout history. We are faced here with a very different problem. The present-day concept is more complex, more pernicious in the light of that colonial pact which still prevails although not openly so called. It assumes that technology has a home country, a capital, a privileged habitat from where it is transferred to the "outer world" subject to conditions which must still remain under supervision.

[6] '' . . . Nature has created a race of workmen, namely the Chinese race, possessed of wondrous manual skill and almost devoid of any feeiing of honour; rule them justly, extracting plentiful returns from them for the benefit of the conquering race, and they will be satisfied; as a race of tillers of the soil you have the negro; be humane and kind to him and everything will be all right; as a race of masters and soldiers there is the European race. Demean that noble race to menial labour like negroes and Chinese and they will rebel. Any rebel among us is more or less a soldier who has missed his career, a creature made for the life heroic on whom you have imposed *a task alien to his race*: a bad workman, too good a soldier. But a life which revolts our workers would make a Chinaman happy, or a fellah, creatures who are in no way military. *If everyone performs the tasks for which he is suited, everything will be fine.*''—(Ernest Renan: "La réforme intellectuelle et morale" in: *Oeuvres complètes*, Paris, Editions Calmann-Levy, 1947, pp. 390, 391.)

Now I am sufficiently naive to believe that we should be talking about exchange of technology, that any transfer of technology should take its place in the framework of pre-acquired know-how, and that the independent technical capacity of each partner is a guarantee of satisfaction in the exchange. I would like to make it plain that the Third World does not start from a total technological vacuum, and that we must watch out for one essential point: the moment one form of technology eliminates another or constitutes a contribution *ex nihilo* the danger arises of an empire being established or, to be more precise, an outside imperial power.

The argument—for there is an argument—in favour of a more cultural technology, meaning one that is taken on and adopted as an expression of our own culture, leads us to start wondering about the present training of our scientists. Short as it was, my career as a teacher prompts me to seek out contacts among schools, colleges and establishments for higher education when I am travelling in different countries. I am constantly discovering to my consternation that in many Third World countries potential senior staff—who were educated not under the colonial system but in our present day when sovereignty is jealously guarded—know more about the mistral than the harmattan wind and spend hours studying the karstic contours while knowing next to nothing about the problems caused by erosion, tropical pedology or laterite formation.

Costly services and wastage of manpower

With regard to doctors, of whom there are unfortunately too few, practical experience of living realities should have increased and extended their knowledge and made them more effective. To give an example of what I mean, Dr. Mahler, the Director General of WHO, noted on 7 April 1977, World Health Day, that more than 80 million children are born in the developing countries every year. Yet with *all the "modern" medical facilities available*, scarcely 4 million of them can be vaccinated against common contagious childhood diseases while more than 5 million die in early childhood.

No development policy can be successful as long as plagues such as malnutrition, bilharziosis, onchocercosis, etc. persist and continue to spread.

The public health infrastructure which we have elected to set up, slavishly following standards which we cannot afford and may not even require, only accentuates inequalities and is of no effect for the greater part of the population. The costs of health care for one of our citizens, as for instance a civil servant, are out of all proportion to the country's budgetary resources. Indeed no figure could in all decency be quoted if one were to include transfers and "health repatriations" [*sic*], doubtless prescribed for excellent reasons, but seriously overloading expenditures on cures to the detriment of expenditures on prevention required for the poorest members of the population. And what about our pharmacopoeias which have enabled millions of town and country patients in China and elsewhere to be given treatment?

We can begin to see clearly the cumulative nature of the vicious circles in which we are caught when we start to calculate how costly it is to keep up this policy of mimicry.

To stick to the field of education, it is well known that many developing countries spend over 25 per cent of their budget on education. But all too often their efforts reach but 10 to 12 per cent of the school age population.

Circumstances being as they are, should a country where the population's annual income is around $100 try to provide the same educational structure in all its forms (and fantasies) as is provided in countries where the average income is ten times greater?

The costs are thus mathematically prohibitive, especially when we keep in mind that the schools have no connection with employment opportunities and become mere factories turning out more unemployed.

If, despite the educational shortcomings, work could be assured for the men who have acquired some knowledge at such cost, there might still be a chance of achieving that profound change which the people are waiting for. But conflicts between generations, ideological battles, tribal warfare both disguised and open, differences between political parties and clans, aberrations of every kind—all lead to irreparable tragedies, to prisons filled with men who could bring life and creativity to the economy and society. Here I must mention the case of my friend Outel Bono[7] and voice my horror of the summary executions which constitute the most serious breach of human rights while at the same time depriving Third World countries of the resources they most need for their development.

Whether it be Outel Bono of the Chad or so many others elsewhere, all such cases of alleged plotting which end in death sentences and sometimes capital punishment are so many shackles placed on the nation's progress in the name of political stability. Can a valid security be found outside the frontiers of reason? And is it the voice of reason to govern graveyards?

It is true that, temporarily, foreign technical assistance does help solve problems caused by lack of skilled personnel in many countries . . . Here I must emphasize the nobleness of any proof of solidarity shown to a people resolved to overcome its problems by its own means and with the help of friends offering their services for a given period. "Brothers without frontiers", those men who devote themselves to a true task of co-operation and solidarity, deserve our admiration and are a needed example.

But I must make a distinction between solidarity of that kind and the form of enterprise which "technical assistance" has become today, about which I have serious reservations.

Some time ago I was a guest at a gathering of Third World students. Two hundred young people aged between 25 and 30, studying to be engineers, doctors, agronomists, civil servants, had come together to discuss their future. Never have I heard such outspoken and disturbing comments, revealing a general attitude towards technical assistance. Here are a few examples:

> I have no faith in the army of "experts" who are unable to fit into any job at home and can only solve their employment problems by going to the developing countries.
>
> I am suspicious of the true motivation of people who take up "Co-operation" in order to get away from personal, marital or

---

[7] Dr. Outel Bono was educated at Toulouse University and was for a long time one of the rare doctors of Chad origin. His competence and devotion were exemplary, as was his patriotism. He was murdered under mysterious circumstances in Paris in August 1973, only a few months before the *coup d'Etat* which overthrew Mr. Tombalbaye, his political foe.

family problems with which they are unable to grapple in their normal social environment. Some of those "co-operators" like the tourists in Mombasa or Banjul have successfully imported all kinds of venal sexual practices hitherto unknown in our societies.

I am opposed to the business of buying equipment with money from co-operation programmes. In the first place, it provides an outlet for the industrial products of the "developed" countries.

I do not accept gifts which end by giving us consumer tastes we cannot satisfy by our own labours and in our own environment.

I am concerned by financial assistance which encourages the purchase of goods which we do not really need and which only push us deeper into debt.

I am revolted by the "telecontrol" of all our policies governing production, distribution, defence, regional associations, as a result of studies done for us by "specialists" . . . whose interests are different from ours and who lead us into ever worsening bondage.

I am against everyone who uses technical assistance to promote a brain drain from the Third World, and all those who deny our leaders, our workers and ourselves the opportunity of using our own critical faculties, our spirit of research, and *our right to rebel*,[8] and who, ignoring the truth and democracy, choose to be surrounded with every kind of mercenary, yellow, black or white, with whose aid they destroy our peoples' liberty.

Some may think that these comments go too far, yet I have heard them coming from men and women at least some of whom will be tomorrow's leaders in one or another of our Third World countries.

---

[8] These italics are mine, and I use them in order to be able to draw parallels in political thought. This may seem surprising but has its importance. To start with, let us remember Abraham Lincoln's thoughts:

"This country, with its institutions, belongs to the people who live in it. When they have had enough of the existing government, they must always be in a position to exercise their constitutional right to censure it or their revolutionary right to overthrow it."

Next to that let us consider the thoughts of Mao Tse-tung:

"Marxism is composed of a multitude of principles, but in the final analysis they can all be reduced to one sentence: *we are right to rebel*."

Their opinions do not speak highly of technical assistance. They regard it as an operation of cultural and political alienation which stifles our ability to resist and our possibilities of developing our homeland.[9]

Today's agricultural policies in the countries concerned do not gainsay those opinions.

The peasant left out in the cold

What every Third World peasant dreams of today, in Asia, Africa as elsewhere, is not so much to improve his situation as *to quit the soil*, in other words to destroy his very existence.

It has become absurd for him not to pursue his chance for "happiness", which is defined in terms of money. You do not make money if you stay a peasant. Experience has shown this, starting with taxation. To make money you must produce what other people want to buy. It is the overseas market which sets the demand: cotton, cocoa, coffee. So you raise cotton, cocoa, coffee. The prices of these commodities keep dropping in comparison with the prices for goods you can buy in exchange: here again it is the foreign market which sets those prices.

We have taught our peasants that, to be "developed", they must acquire goods which are bought in exchange for cash crops. This is a fallacy which deceives them and makes them slaves to money.

We have made it the fashion for each person to own a car. We have resolved that the ideal home must have a tin roof, even if you die of heat beneath it. To manufacture these new products, local and

[9] This recalls a pertinent study made by François Perroux in one of his basic works, *L'économie du XXe siècle* (Paris, P.U.F., 3rd edition, 1969), p. 401, where he says: "A victorious nation sends food and medical aid to the conquered inhabitants. The dominant economy helps its partners with their reconstruction programmes. Colonialism no longer dares to be recognized as such and to come out in the open: it arranges for its partial survival by proclaiming the need for co-operation . . ."
In opposition to such technical assistance of "perdition" I set forth resolutely the Solidarity Contract, to which I shall revert later, based on independent decisions, on the work of our people, their self-reliance and their determination to participate in a civilization of "the human condition experienced together and shared together"— all that within the framework of a strategy for satisfying basic needs, including the fight for peace and freedom.

imported goods are required, as well as a lot of work. All that costs money.

The hoe and the machete alone will not produce such money for the peasant, not even enough for a slight improvement of his level of consumption. He can see no reason to subject his children to the same fate. Cost what it may, he is bent on imitating others. So he consents to destroy his way of life. And most independent governments are only too ready to help him do so.

Since coffee has to be produced for export, lots of it, more land is needed to produce on a scale which will satisfy our ambitions.

Even with the help of a co-operative it is costly to acquire specially selected seed, fertilizers and fungicides, tractors and imported tools. Loan systems only serve to drive the farmers into debt, and sometimes they become victims of usury. For example, take a planter with a 50-acre farm who wants to replace some of his coffee bushes with new ones. It will require the income of 4 years of his crop to repay his loan. The risks involved in transactions of this nature are all too obvious, so great, in fact, that many peasants find themselves obliged to sell their land and go to work for a wage for others who are more fortunate; or else they are forced to migrate to city slums.

Agriculture thus becomes a "traditional" occupation only for marginal areas outside the flow of world trade, like in certain countries in West Africa which have no outlet to the sea. Everywhere else, rudimentary types of agriculture, which are characterized by low productivity and income, are on their way out.

On the other hand a highly technical form of farming is developing. In Latin America you find more and more large and medium-sized holdings being operated along the most up-to-date lines.

Whenever a crop of speculative nature is left in peasants' hands, people are inclined to conclude that it is hard to make it pay with modern methods. But that is only temporary. Even plantations where traditional methods could produce good results are threatened by foreign intervention. In Colombia, for instance, coffee was grown by peasant families who owned or leased the ground on mountain sides where no tractor could be used. The peasant families had acquired a high degree of skill at raising their crops and treating the grain. In addition, peasants did not reckon their work and that of their families at its true value. Export firms even interfered in that system. They turned the small family production into a "paying" enterprise, monopolizing the marketing of the grain and taking advantage of the change to a monetary economy.

In order to pay the moneylender, the land-owner, or the tax collector, the peasants are thus forced to go in for speculative crops to be sold on world markets, to the detriment of their own food crops. Again in Colombia, where 70 per cent of the coffee growers are small farmers with only 20 per cent of the plantations in their hands, there has been an increasing food shortage in recent years, according to official reports. One of the causes has been the extension of the land given over to coffee growing.

"In the old days", says an aged peasant, "you could not sell bananas. There were too many around. There was enough for everybody. Today we have to buy this basic food on the market, and prices are constantly rising."

Village folk are no longer as self-sustaining as they used to be, thanks to monetarization. Peasants are obliged to sell their produce under appalling conditions just to cover what they are made to pay, and have to *buy their food*.

Josué de Castro already brought this out in his book *Géopolitique de la faim* (*Geopolitics of Hunger*): it was the dislocation of traditional social structures and the domination of, first, the colonial powers and *later the indigenous notables* that were responsible for aggravating the problems of food shortages.

Is famine spreading?

There is another tragic side of this policy of profits at any cost. I refer to the wastage to be seen on all sides and in every form. The land is being used in such a way that it is being ruined for ever in the space of a few years.

It is well known that in Africa, vast areas of what was once dense forest are now covered with a hard shell of laterite extending for hundreds of thousands of square miles.

In the Sahel area, the desert has been advancing partly because of the extension of new acreages being planted with ground-nut and partly owing to excessive cattle raising (a country like Senegal is almost entirely dependent on the export of ground-nuts). Besides, it is easier to collect taxes from a settled population than from nomads. The colonial powers and their successors did in fact attempt to settle the nomadic Fulah and the Tuareg. Attracted by the wells sunk at the edges of the desert, the latter merely raised more cattle, which to them means status and wealth.

The consequent overcropping impoverished the vegetable topsoil, resulting in profound qualitative changes in the composition of the flora. Plants liked by herbivorous animals no longer have time to grow if there are too many animals cropping the area. Perennials are destroyed and their places taken by annuals, whose roots do not go so deep so that they hold the soil less well. To these factors must be added the damage done by goats, which tear up the young plant.

The disaster which occurred as a result of a period of exceptional drought was to be foreseen.

It is forecast that desertification in countries of the Sahel area, like Niger, will be still worse in 30 years' time. In that area, for instance, only three different types of vegetable plants can be found today growing on a given hectare, three stunted little shrubs, although peasants still remember playing in the woods on the same spot less than three decades ago.

Yet we are all aware of the tremendous gravity of the consequences of such ignorance of our geography and such indifference to our natural environment.

One is undoubtedly impressed by the technical level of the development plans which every Third World country is now drawing up or is obliged to submit, with the aid of experts who are in general competent and frequently devoted to their task. But invariably we find that all such plans lack social purpose, particularly where agriculture is concerned. Nowhere will you find it laid down how producing cotton, coffee or cocoa is going to make it possible to satisfy directly a given number of peasant families' basic needs in food, housing, health, education.[10] On that point, the problem is covered by a single sentence

[10] Still more dramatic are the consequences of the evacuation towards the coast and the production of certain minerals like phosphates. Beaches and vegetation are polluted, fish decimated. The GNP may be growing, but the fisherman's family is getting poorer since what they need for food now has to be imported.

or a paragraph, referring for instance to the items in the budget for social security, the latest magic word for extending and concealing privileges, to which the peasant has no right.

If I emphasize the incoherence of development plans so far as the peasants are concerned, it is in order to highlight another kind of fraud.

Agricultural exports are increasing fast in all Third World countries. Yet incomes are constantly going down. Worse still, the production of coffee, cocoa, tea, cotton, jute, oleaginous plants, none of which is directly involved in the population's "basic needs", is rising much faster than that of basic cereals.

The pattern of consumption in the West is becoming so widespread that the demand for wheat, which we do not produce, is rising and the Third World is becoming more and more dependent on imports for food.[11]

A new expression has been devised to denote the strategy of importing foodstuffs: telenourishment. Many of our countries are now subjected to that dangerous obligation in one form or another. Some have to appeal for aid at more or less irregular intervals in view of their poor capacity to pay; other wealthier countries, such as those who can produce and export oil, have resolved to buy their food "since the money is available". In any case there are very few countries which, due to their capacity to feed themselves, are able to avoid having to resort to telenourishment.

In such cases, recent or long-established industrial monoculture is a real tragedy. In this connection A. Provent and F. de Ravignan tell of two striking examples, in Cameroon and Upper Volta: "It is extremely interesting", they write, "to compare a village in the cocoa area of southern Cameroon, long addicted to dairy farming, with one in western Upper Volta where they have recently started growing cotton."

In the former, they tell us, "the average annual household income is around CFA Frs. 2000; in the latter it is about CFA Frs. 600. In the Cameroon village most of the huts have tin roofs and almost all

---

[11] In some countries bread made from wheat is increasingly taking the place of maize or millet cakes (I take this up again in the next chapter).

the children can read, as against 10 per cent in the Upper Volta village. But one thing is certain: both suffer equally from malaria, worms, tetanus, venereal diseases, infantile undernourishment. . . . What is the point in being literate if one is destitute?''[12] It is easy to see why reports like that recently prompted Amadou Ahidjo, the President of the United Republic of Cameroon, to call for an international enquiry into the social implications of economic development projects.[13] For destitution pursues or threatens us because we failed to choose poverty. Huge plantations, modern farming techniques, more intensive production, higher sales figures . . . all those only give us money. Money steadily devalues and cannot be of use to all, but only to the few. The peasant has not died out, but he surely will, especially if, as occasionally happens, we start building dams for irrigation and then make no use of them.

The illusions of industrialization

Voltaire once warned us of the importance of freeing ourselves from three great evils: "boredom, vice and need".

If you talk with a political leader in a developing country and ask him what are his most immediate concerns, he will very seldom fail to bring up the idleness of the young and the consequent need of investments for setting up industries, saying that creating jobs in industry seems the ultimate solution in the face of the rural exodus, unemployment, prostitution and delinquency.

But very early in the conversation you will note that the model of an industrial society also arouses serious misgivings and scarcely concealed disillusion.

That immediately raises two questions: how is industrialization carried out? What are its social consequences?

In the first place, it has frequently been stressed that the industrial countries retain the sectors with high added value, and transfer certain

[12] A. Provent and F. de Ravignan: *Le nouvel ordre de la faim, révolutions paysannes* (Paris, Editions du Seuil, 1977).

[13] A joint project undertaken by the IILS and the German Federal Ministry for Economic Co-operation.

of their activities to the Third World through the multinational corporations, which are the real decision-makers as regards the "international division of labour" and its evolution.

Three basic reasons for this transfer can be noted. Firstly, it proves profitable to move labour-intensive industries, as it helps "export" social problems and benefits from the wage differential between two groups of countries. Of course at the moment this form of transfer is suffering restrictions thanks to the unemployment prevailing in the West, but at least two sectors are still involved: textiles and electronic assembly. The world's markets are flooded with transistors "made in Hong Kong", pocket calculators "made in Taiwan", television sets "made in Singapore". This redeployment took place fairly spontaneously 10 years ago, the multinationals having decided freely the industrial policy of the countries into which they moved, where they found substantial benefits: plentiful labour, unemployment keeping wages down, and especially a high degree of manual skill among the workers, the heritage of cultures which had been technically advanced for centuries.

A second reason for the transfer was the trend in industrialized countries to re-structure their industries into smaller production units where man would no longer be the slave of the machine. Two other points in favour of the trend were that it helped to avoid pollution, which new legislation is now making so costly, and that it was economically beneficial because plants were being set up adjacent to the sources of raw materials.

Other sectors have thus been affected by the redeployment: the first processing of metals (metallurgy of iron and steel) and of products for energetics (petrochemistry). A feature of this last is the high level of technology required. In this case it is the availability not of plentiful cheap labour that is sought, but of highly qualified workers, which in most cases entails resorting to technical assistance.

The third reason for transferring operations is the increasing purchasing power to acquire manufactured products in the Third World countries themselves. This new development, plus the prior existence of an industrial base, lies behind the rise of import-substituting industries: agricultural food processing, clothing and, later, electrical equipment, automobile manufacture, etc. At one time it was thought that these sectors would grow rapidly. It has now been discovered, however, that the home market is strictly limited since only a minority can afford to buy most of these durable consumer goods. In the same way "import-substitution" has proved disappointing as far as employment is concerned, for the technology is often "sophisticated" in these sectors as well, and is not suited to the simple manpower available. The incompatibility between technology and employment is not always apparent; indeed, it often shows up only after irreversible decisions have been taken.

Even in Brazil, a privileged country which possesses a wide range of this kind of industry, there is concern that only 17 per cent of the active population is employed in the manufacturing industry whereas the urban population has gone up 30 to 60 per cent in 15 years.[14] It is worth keeping this in mind at a time when there is so much talk about "geographical redeployment of industry".

As we have just seen, the latter is in fact carried out in accordance with the interests of the industrial countries. The Third World's sole participation consists of taking in a heterogeneous and disjointed collection of industrial sectors: petrochemistry and steel in the Middle East, electronics in South-East Asia and automobile assembly in some Latin American countries, textiles in Africa and Asia. Such industries are introduced piecemeal by sector, and geared towards foreign markets.

It is important also to examine the costs for the receiving countries. Substantial loans have enabled some States to set up factories producing goods for equipment. A World Bank study shows that the foreign debt of 84 developing countries almost doubled between 1969 and 1973, rising from $62.5 billion to $116.8 billion. In 1976 the figure reached $212.6 billion. In 7 years external debt had thus risen 3.4 times at a rate which has been growing since the 1973 economic turning point.[15]

Operating in a state of under-capacity for production is often due to poor equipment—which in certain cases is out of date, worn out and in

[14] *Géographie du sous-développement* by Yves Lacoste (Paris, P.U.F., 1965).

[15] See Appendix I for currently available statistics on developing countries with low and medium incomes.

constant need of repair; or, on the contrary, in other instances the high technological level of some new equipment is poorly adapted to the skill structure of the workforce, and this gives rise to frequent production breakdowns. Whatever be its cause, it is the failure to master manufacturing methods that lies behind the excessive production costs: repair and maintenance costs, financial charges, depreciation and in certain countries the high cost of energy.

Producing under these conditions lowers the competitivity of locally made products which are beyond the people's low purchasing power. Thus many of these plants, as in Africa for instance, are turning out goods which cost more than the imported product, much to the people's astonishment.

The multinationals hand over units which cease to be profitable, or make up for the losses with tax facilities and low wages. Then they reconvert to new sectors. Their capital is thus quickly recovered with the help of national development banks, which continue to finance such projects for their own "local counterparts", and Governments, which continue granting tax favours.

In the final analysis, the aim is to produce at minimum cost, so minimal that profits are often 10 to 20 times greater than those of the parent company in, say, Europe. The chart facing gives the comparative advantages and shows the calculations.

An industrial development strategy of this kind encourages a new form of alliance between indigenous and foreign privileged minorities. They export the capital derived from the profits of the industry and later bring them in again under the guise of foreign investments, which once again take advantage of the favourable conditions established for the purpose.

From infernal work to destructive urbanization . . .

This brings us to the social consequences of these phenomena of industrialization.

The social situation of the new industrial workers is worrying, to say the least. Strict discipline is imposed on them: to make the investments worthwhile there must be no question of trade union rights,

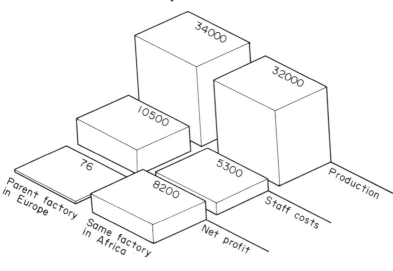

The industrialists' calculations

The above figures refer to the case of a clothing factory in its fifth year of operations. In the European hypothesis, it concerns an existing plant, bought back by an investor: taxes on profits are at the rate of 50%. In the African hypothesis the plant was set up from scratch with favourable capital, mainly loaned over 10 years by a development fund. Its size is the same as its European competitor's (350 workers at the start). Growth is the same (+10% p.a.). Its sales go to the same market, Europe. But there is an appreciable difference: staff costs half as much and profits are tax-free for 5 years (after that they are taxed at 30%). The conclusion to be drawn is obvious.
(*Economia*, No. 19, January 1976.)

---

strikes, collective bargaining. Human rights must not be exercised to the detriment of the investor's interests. One politician as recently as 1972 suggested that our embassies abroad should be judged by the amount of investments they succeeded in obtaining, *"no matter what the conditions attached"*.

Some governments spare no effort in their desire to see their people entering wholesale into the industrial era. But recycling the rural masses for jobs in industry is a painful process. Life in the slums or rents falling due, the agonized search for employment, the infernal rhythm of work, are all such sudden changes that they not infrequently lead to suicide.

One factor provides a particularly good indication of the extent and speed of the change: the urban housing index. It is known that when many countries, particularly in Asia, become industrialized, the new housing areas are often taken over by the middle classes as rents are too high for the industrial workers' purchasing power. In some countries, there is a deliberate policy of destroying traditional forms of life and culture, just like in Europe. Singapore appears to have been an extreme case of that tragic mimicry, as shown in a recent report:[16] "Between 1960 and 1975, the State built 250,000 dwellings, and 55% of Singapore's 2.3 million inhabitants have already been rehoused with public funds. Between now and 1980, a further 150,000 new dwellings will be constructed and 70% of the population will be housed in these State-owned buildings. Simultaneously with the erection of these satellite cities, the Government is systematically tearing down traditional houses and small villages with a view to the social rehabilitation of their inhabitants. . . . As it lays down the living style of the population, the Government is at the same time severely cutting down its growth. There are heavy taxes of various kinds on families with more than two children. One of the purposes is to stabilize the population at 3.5 million by the beginning of the next century. The state lodgings, mostly with three rooms, are meant to house a nuclear family of the Western type. Clan families in Chinese style cannot find shelter there. Finally, this way of rehousing the population doubtless makes for a more efficient social control."

So industrialization, if badly carried out, leads to a destructive form of urbanization, aggravating further the contradictions and social inequalities, as it emerges from the different patterns of consumption.

Those who get richer, the upper middle classes, well-to-do tradesmen, civil servants, all generally scorn goods which are locally made, and impose Western standards of consumer taste. Their lavish spending is so much lost to national savings, so much gained for foreign capital. In recent years observers have noted, and particularly Jean Ziegler,[17] the increasing funds from the Third World put into European banks,

[16] Jean-Luc Lederey: "Singapour ou la lutte pour le progrès", *Journal de Genève*, 17-21 February 1977.

[17] See *Une Suisse au-dessus de tout soupçon* (Paris, Editions du Seuil, 1976).

particularly since the beginning of "the crisis". Corruption is often flagrant. Who has not heard the story of the "castle of drought" in one of the countries plagued by famine?

The cities in the Third World are the living expression of that society of accumulation, exaggeration, piling up, corruption. Over the last 25-30 years they have been mushrooming at an extraordinary rate. Urban population in Asia rose from 180 million in 1950 to 575 million today; in Latin America from 50 to 160 million; in Africa from 30 to 90 million. *The cities are the cancer, swelling and consuming the entire body.* They take land from the countryside, suck in the worker and his income, but they do not give him back any vitality. Geographical experts demonstrate that modern-type cities are like a foreign body in "underdeveloped" countries. Such cities depend little on the surrounding countryside for their food, which is sold in the city markets, where most of the produce comes from abroad.

In Africa, the number of cars and lorries in circulation has gone up from 3.4 million in 1967 to 5.2 million in 1972; in Latin America, from 7 to 16 million and in Asia (excluding Japan), from 3 to 6 million. The smallest countries are no exception. Maseru has more private cars than Peking. It seems to have been forgotten that every private car sold deprives hundreds of people of a decent public transport system, and every private refrigerator sold puts off the day of the community freezer.

In residential areas people vie for luxury: air-conditioning, various gadgets, all are considered indispensable. There are more and more swimming pools and larger lawns, all taking water away from the poorer districts. As prices for land keep rising, the poor are crowded together in the most unpleasant areas.

In a study carried out for the International Labour Office, P. Bairoch[18] estimates that the number of urban unemployed in all the developing countries together rose, between 1950 and 1970, from 7 to 22 million, or from 2 to 3.5 per-cent of the total labour force, but from 10 to 12 per cent of the urban labour force. Among young people between 15 and 24 years of age, the unemployment rate is twice that of the population as a whole.

[18] *Le chômage urbain dans les pays en voie de développement* (Geneva, 1972).

A vast marginal population does its best to "make out" by living in the shadow of the wealthier districts. In Santiago they say "Nos ayudamos" ("We help ourselves").

The big city, the European or American type of megalopolis, has become the "image" to which we aspire—and our illusion. I see nothing very edifying or exemplary about those tribes on a permanent war footing who fill Chicago and its suburbs. The first sophism derives from the fact that we define development without taking account of the environment: but good environment is the prime condition for developing since it enables us to lead a well-balanced life. At present, the diversity of ecosystems which mark man's habitat is becoming more and more reduced: we create entirely artificial urban areas, we give rural areas a uniformity, sometimes deface them by the extension of industrial monoculture over vast zones; we destroy the last traces of natural growth, push back the forests, eliminate areas which we do not believe we can use, like marshes. As to the biomass of non-domesticated animals, it has virtually ceased to exist in the "developed" regions of the world. The finality of expansion and maximum industrial growth, which has been raised to the status of a dogma by the Western mind and economic thought, has rightly been denounced by contemporary ecologists. No living species may exploit the natural environment and ignore both the laws of replacement of the elements removed and the rate of perpetuation of the biocenoses, that is the conservation of the biological equilibrium between the animal and vegetable worlds. Any human community which consumes more from its eco-system than the latter can produce is eating up both the interest and the capital. Is this not the road to destruction?

The tragedy of lost sense

Comparison does not necessarily get at the truth . . . but I cannot help recalling here a book which made its mark at one time: *The Lonely Crowd, a Study of the Changing American Character* by David Riesman, which came out 25 years ago. The author noted that as America's social development progressed faster, values changed so rapidly that, rather than trust to the "gyroscopes" of their own principles implanted within them, people were beginning to put their faith in their "radar screens", adopting new directions and constantly changing their route to conform to the tastes, opinions and values of those whom they sought to imitate.

Whole nations are going through somewhat the same kind of process. Many a Third World country, telecontrolled from abroad and incapable of following the inner principles of self-direction, is today obliged to rely on radar. Every pilot surrounded by fog or storm knows that "radar time" is a perilous time. And when the radar itself is out of order, it appears that the fatal moment has come.

I called this chapter "The Folly of Mimicry". Mime was the last form of Roman comedy. The actors wore neither brodekin nor buskin and they painted their faces.

Is the play in which we have chosen to act really a comedy? Elsewhere[19] I referred to "tragic mimicry". Walking on one's hands is indeed a form of acrobatics reserved for those who specialize in that kind of thing. For them, as for everyone else, if this acrobatic feat becomes a regular way of life, it is not merely uncomfortable, it is a real torture. It is true that such torture may constitute an opportunity by the very challenge it offers. Nietzsche used to say "Only something that hurts really badly takes full grip on a man's whole being and speeds up the process of his spirit bursting in on him".

The story of the "Mad sheep" (still more money and still more women) did not end happily . . . but fortunately the history of man may come to a different ending. When we have finished piling up our pleasures and our decorations, when our men of law and our scientists have shown off their ceremonial robes far and wide and we have made the world laugh at our buffoonery, there will still be children with sunken eyes asking us to account for the dead bodies picked up at dawn off the streets of Calcutta and for the women in black standing in the twilight of the hills of the Tigris silently calling for the innocent to be avenged.

And I can assure you it will hurt, it will really hurt badly. Maybe then the spirit will burst in upon us.

We must, without delay, open our eyes anew and think again.

---

[19] *La formation des cadres africains en vue de la croissance économique* by Albert Tévoédjrè, with preface by Alfred Sauvy (Paris, Diloutremer, 1965).

CHAPTER III

Rethinking the Economy

"He who borrows to marry
Shall sell his children
To pay the interest."
Lebanese proverb.

"The best state for human nature is that in which, while no one is poor, no one desires to be richer, nor has any reason to fear being thrust back by the efforts of others to push themselves forward."
(John Stuart Mill: *Principles of Political Economy*, 1852, Book IV, Chapter VI, para. 2.)

Everybody knows the story of Diogenes who was once found in the streets of Athens in broad daylight holding a lighted lantern and saying: "I am looking for an honest man."

May I be forgiven if, in our times when great talents abound, I, in turn, take up the search for some honest economists?

And yet it is tempting—in the face of the indescribable poverty, which we know exists, the unemployment which is flooding the most affluent societies, inflation and rampant disorder—to suggest that a new "General Theory of Economics" is what we most need.

Towards an inductive logic: priority to reality

Descartes used to point out that we are the victims of two main sources of error: our "appetites" and our "teachers".

We have seen how an imperfect control over our appetites has brought us anything but well-being.

When I say that it is necessary to encourage those who are able to rethink economics, I should like to lay stress on the responsibility of our teachers and recall the syllogism which we have already referred to, which is the twin brother of the "syllogism of desire"[1] propounded by Aristotle. I think that it clearly expresses the mimicry which is our fatal error.

Indeed, it is high time to challenge the arguments of the advocates of a deductive reasoning which is based on hypotheses that are of doubtful validity or have never been proved by experience.

We have been led into the worst imaginable dilemmas by placing our confidence in economic arguments which have spread round the world theorems and laws, the truth of which only remained to be demonstrated by each party playing their appointed role. I need only mention, for example, the arguments concerning the mono-cultures of the "periphery" which enable the "centre" to live comfortably on differentiated and complementary products but leave those who believed in a remunerative exchange to starve.

The premises of the economic thinking by which most of the countries of the Third World are guided are formulated elsewhere, *regardless of where that* "elsewhere" may be; that is a fact but it is also a great misfortune.

For the foundation of deductive logic, as we learn from philosophy, is the principle of identity. Once this is established and accepted, we are caught in the trap. Having affirmed one proposition, we have no right to affirm another which contradicts it, and so we find ourselves duty-bound, once having affirmed it, to affirm it at all times, with all its consequences.

Another great misfortune is that the men of the Third World are slow to adopt a new kind of thinking—*on their own initiative*—which is based on another and more valid type of reasoning than the former, namely, induction.

In an operation of formal logic, in fact, deduction has no more force than the weakest argument—*Pejorem sequitur semper conclusio partem*. Deduction from external objectives which are defined by the "teacher" is leading the countries of the Third World to false or

---

[1] Desire says "I am thirsty"; "Here is something to drink" says sensation or imagination, or intelligence, and the animal immediately drinks. (*De motu animalium*.)

[2] Schopenhauer derived a precept from the same principle which is well known today: "Never let somebody else establish your own truth. More than of anything else, be ashamed of doing that."

negative conclusions.[2] On the other hand, it is obvious that induction, based on the actual realities to be found in our countries, has a broadening effect, that it increases the ways, means and quality of our judgement, that it takes us from the particular to the universal, and, above all, from what is merely contingent to what is really necessary.

It was Francis Bacon who made the "Hunt of Pan" famous. It consisted of a systematic collection of the most widely varied experiments. Japan, for example, has engaged in a real "Hunt of Pan" in the attempt to build up its industrial power. In their study entitled *Towards a New Kind of Co-operation*,[3] Yves Berthelot and Giulio Fossi have drawn attention to that country's prodigious efforts to organize the dissemination of knowledge: all the technical books and reviews which are being published in the industrialized countries are received and collected. "Every review is analyzed, the articles are classified, and a summary of every subject, translated into Japanese, is sent out to all industrialists who might be interested in it. Between 3,000 and 5,000 engineers are engaged in preparing these abstracts, and they also answer inquiries from industrialists who want their advice about the methods used in manufacturing certain products or increasing the efficiency of a certain manufacturing process."

Of course, we may have serious doubts about the wisdom of directing this prodigious effort towards the systematic conquest of foreign markets. My only point is that Japan is trying to pierce the secret of the technological principle, to understand and assimilate it and to develop its possible applications through its own efforts.

"Rethinking" the economy therefore means, first of all, to carry out a thorough cultural revision, to undertake a critique of the dominating pattern of knowledge so as to restore to its full rights a kind of reasoning which is rooted in and sustained by experience. By combining—as Kant already suggested—the principles of substance, causality and reciprocal action, we obtain a scientific method which will not necessarily favour the quantification of goods or incomes but will in any case ensure the real transformation of the Gross National Product into what Toynbee calls the "Gross National

---

[3] Yves Berthelot and Giulio Fossi: *Pour une nouvelle coopération* (Paris, P.U.F., 1975).

Welfare" (the welfare of individual human beings and whole peoples).

We have to go back to the very foundations of economic science and change a few of its implicit premises, such as the priority of the egotistic struggle for existence. Economic knowledge must be built not on premises of the will to power and the search for profit but on premises of the sound organization of the life of human groups, in accordance with the very etymology of the word "economy". By putting profits first and favouring mercantile trading, economics has been reduced to mere "chrematistics", that is the art of making money.

We must, therefore, reclaim our right to break free from this kind of geocentrism which has been imposed on us, and of which Raoul Prebisch and Samir Amin, among others, have given an apt description[4] and we must promote our own "intelligible heliocentrism" as Copernicus discovered and taught long ago. Intelligible, because we will first have observed every social reality in its specificity and then have reflected on these situations. "The fact suggests the idea, the idea directs the experiment, the experiment judges the idea." These are the words of Claude Bernard, but they could equally well be a reference to Ibn Khaldun. Though the latter, alas, had very little understanding of the psychology and customs of the black African Negro peoples, he was one of the very first to emphasize, in his Muqaddima, the influence of geographic, ethnic and socio-economic factors on the development of civilizations.

Everything becomes possible, therefore, if we start from reason, no longer reason *in posse* but *in esse*—I mean to say not merely theoretical but tested in practice on the basis of real facts which have been directly experienced by the peoples themselves and within geometrical limits which are not alien to them. Some hope does exist, in fact, since the United Nations General Assembly has undertaken to promote the establishment of a new international economic order.

It was with this in mind that an Association of the Economists of the Third World was created, whose first Congress was held at Algiers

---

[4] For a critical analysis of this kind of geocentrism, see, in particular: S. Amin: *L'accumulation à l'échelle mondiale* (Paris, Editions Anthropos, 1974) and R. Prebisch: "Commercial Policy in the Underdeveloped Countries", in *American Economic Review*, Vol. 49, No. 2, May 1959, Papers and Proceedings, pp. 251-73.

in February 1976. The preliminary results are promising,[5] and it is to be hoped that its work will be further intensified following this initial phase. It is important that we exchange ideas with those who, on behalf of the Third World, are propounding theories and working out the methodology of a new kind of economy, by telling them about our own observations, remarks and anxieties, so that they can better understand the realities facing us.

Return to use value: auto-production and the service economy

The point I should like to stress is that the theory of the pursuit of affluence is erroneous if it deprives us of a need we feel every day, namely, the need to try to construct some other economic theory for a society based on anti-consumption, a society of collective wealth and participation in a poverty which will mean the greater welfare of the greatest number.

"Rethinking" the economy is, in fact, to return to the source of the concept itself; it is to favour social needs rather than productivity for the benefit of monopolies; it is to try to put an end to the social deficiencies created by the scarcity of goods which are essential for the survival of every individual and mankind as a whole.

Relying on these basic ideas and on the methodology referred to above, I think it possible to find satisfactory answers to such fundamental questions as the following:

What is our situation in the world today? What kind of human and social condition are we in?

If, generally speaking, every economy is based on some form of production which is the foundation of the nation's wealth, then what should be produced, for whom and how?

How should the world economy be organized so that the wealth of the privileged nations will not be a cause of world poverty?

At the Conference of the Club of Rome held at Algiers in October

[5] See the *Report of the Congress of the Third World Economists Association*, Algiers, 1976.

1976 to discuss the RIO project,[6] a Chinese professor, Mr. Han-Sheng Lin, gave a talk which attracted the attention of all the participants. "Do we want to construct an economic system?", he said. "Well then, let's take a look at our peoples. Who are they? There are many of them. They are poor, under-nourished, badly housed, uneducated, sick, victims of unemployment. There is our starting-point. There could not be any other." Indeed, I believe that this is the foundation of any search for an economic policy. And it should be emphasized that these peoples, our peoples, are living in a world, in a geographic, geo-political and socio-cultural environment, which determines how they live and which therefore must be organized.

We venture to hope that these simple and primary truths will constitute the basic principles of "our little book". By giving them practical effect, we will be able to give new directions to our agriculture and industry, improve our terms of trade with the outside world and above all provide ourselves with a use value that is *absolutely essential*.

The exchange economy, whether regulated by the market or by planning, is necessary at all levels if it is accepted that specialization is required for certain activities in order to increase their productivity. However, it should not be allowed to eliminate the production of goods for direct use by the producers themselves. Moreover, there must be room for what might be called a true service economy, not, as has hitherto been thought, the result but the actual source of development. Top priority should be given to the organization of social services in the most disadvantaged regions, and in no case can we wait for them to be established as a "spinoff", once industrialization is largely under way. After all, they serve to meet basic needs in the same way as the most useful material goods. In addition, these services—health, housing, functional infrastructure, universal training and education—are indispensable for the rapid and widespread improvement of work capabilities. An economy of this kind, which furnishes direct services, promotes use value[7] and at the same time its

[6] RIO Project: *Reshaping the International Order*, Report prepared under the direction of Jan Tinbergen (New York, Dutton, 1976).

[7] It is not, therefore, a matter of the systematic "tertiarization" of society, which is widely and rightly deplored in many industrialized countries.

Rethinking the Economy

activities benefit the greatest number of people. Such a principle calls for a simple and inexpensive technology, of a "grass-roots" nature, a flexible and diversified range of qualifications, management and financing which are administered, at least in part, by the communities themselves, in short, a decentralized organization—the village in rural areas, the district in urban areas—graduated according to appropriate scales of proximity and membership in the various social groups.

In this way, "rethinking the economy" is to make it consubstantial with the social order. Market value and production for the market will then no longer be the goals and criteria of the economy as a whole.

Where do we stand?

However, these ideas ought to be confirmed by looking at a map of the world: what, in fact, is our situation? How do others see us?

Even the best statistics often have serious defects. However, I think that if we want to have some idea of the reasons for rethinking our economy, we must take a good look at ourselves and try to understand ourselves better.

I suggest, therefore, that the reader study the figures on the facing page which I am submitting for analysis and which are indicators of economic and social development by groups of countries (low income, medium income, high income).

In particular, this table shows that for about fifty of the poorest countries, which already include one-third of mankind, the situation is absolutely catastrophic all along the line.

A few brief comments might be added to these figures.

Not only is the gap between the different regions of the world wide, but when it is measured by the numerous indicators we have at our disposal, it is seen to be constantly deepening too. As far as wealth and opportunities are concerned, it is a gap which exists not only *between* nations but also *within* the nations themselves.

In 1974, more than a hundred developing countries in Africa, Asia and Latin America (with 67 per cent of the world population) together accounted for only 14 per cent of the total world product; on the other hand, the 25 industrialized countries of Europe and North

Economic and social indicators of development, by groups of countries

	Popu-lation, mid-1976	Per capita GNP, 1974	Physical quality of life index (PQLI)[e]	Per capita GNP growth rate, 1965-74	Birth rate, per 1000	Death rate, per 1000	Life expec-tancy at birth	Infant mortality per 1000 live births	Literacy	Per capita public education expend's, 1973	Per capita mili-tary expend's, 1973	Total exports, f.o.b., 1975	Total imports, c.i.f., 1975	Inter-national reserves, Sept. 1976
	(mil.)	*($)*	*(%)*				*(years)*			*($)*	*($)*	*($ mil.)*	*($ mil.)*	*($ mil.)*
ⱽ-income countries ᵣse with *per capita* GNP ᵉᵣ $300); 48 countries[a]	1341.3	152	39	1.7	40	17	48	134	33	3	6	27,143	32,809	13,869
ᵛᵉʳ middle-income countries ᵣse with *per capita* GNP of ᴐ-$699); 39 countries[b]	1145.4	338	59	4.4	30	11	61	70	34	10	17	37,828	48,835	13,015
ᵘᵉʳ middle-income countries ᵣse with *per capita* GNP of ᴐ-$1999); 35 countries[c]	470.6	1091	67	4.7	36	10	61	82	65	28	31	104,821	114,129	39,193
ʰ-income countries ᵣse with *per capita* GNP of ᴐ0 or more); 37 countries[d]	1057.0	4361	95	4.0	17	9	71	21	97	217	232	687,478	680,253	175,967

ᶠghanistan, Bangladesh, Benin (ex-Dahomey), Bhutan, Bolivia, Botswana, Burma, Burundi, Cambodia, Central African ᴐire, Chad, Comoros, Democratic Yemen, Egypt, Equatorial Guinea, Ethiopia, Gambia, Guinea, Haiti, India, Indonesia, ᵧa, Lesotho, Macao, Madagascar, Malawi, Maldives, Mali, Mauritania, Nepal, Niger, Nigeria, Pakistan, Republic of Laos, ₐnda, Sierra Leone, Sikkim, Socialist Republic of Viet-Nam, Somalia, Sri Lanka, Sudan, Tanzania, Togo, Tonga, Uganda, ₑr Volta, Yemen, Zaire.

ᵇania, Cameroon, Cape Verde, China, Colombia, Congo, Cuba, Dominican Republic, Ecuador, El Salvador, Ghana, ₙada, Guatemala, Guinea-Bissau, Guyana, Honduras, Ivory Coast, Jordan, Liberia, Malaysia, Mauritius, Mongolia, ᵒcco, Mozambique, Nicaragua, Papua-New Guinea, Paraguay, People's Democratic Republic of Korea, Philippines, ₐblic of Korea, Saõ Tomé and Principe, Senegal, Southern Rhodesia, Swaziland, Syrian Arab Republic, Thailand, Tunisia, ₜern Samoa, Zambia.

ᵍeria, Angola, Argentina, Barbados, Brazil, Bulgaria, Chile, Costa Rica, Cyprus, Fiji, Formosa, Guadeloupe, Hong Kong, , Iraq, Jamaica, Lebanon, Malta, Martinique, Mexico, Netherlands Antilles, Oman, Panama, Peru, Portugal, Republic ₐbon, Reunion, Romania, South Africa, Surinam, Trinidad and Tobago, Turkey, Uruguay, Venezuela, Yugoslavia.

ᵤstralia, Austria, Bahamas, Bahrain, Belgium, Canada, Czechoslovakia, Denmark, Federal Republic of Germany, Finland, ₙce, German Democratic Republic, Greece, Hungary, Iceland, Ireland, Israel, Italy, Japan, Kuwait, Libyan Arab Jamahiriya, ₑmburg, Netherlands, New Zealand, Norway, Poland, Puerto Rico, Qatar, Saudi Arabia, Singapore, Spain, Sweden, ₜzerland, United Arab Emirates, United Kingdom, United States, USSR.

ₐch country's PQLI (Physical Quality of Life Index) rating is based on an average of its index ratings for life expectancy, ₙt mortality, and literacy in the mid-1970s.

ᵒte: The data given for each income-group are cumulative totals for population, exports, imports and international reserve ᵣes, and averages weighted by mid-1976 populations for all other indicators.

ᵒurce: Statistics taken from Overseas Development Council, *The U.S. and World Development; Agenda for Action 1977*, New ₖ, Praeger, 1977, and drawn up mainly on the basis of the series published by the International Monetary Fund, the World ₖ, the United States Agency for International Development, UNESCO and UNCTAD.

America (with only 25 per cent of the world population) accounted for almost 72 per cent of the total GNP for the same year.

In spite of the variety of ways of defining and evaluating poverty in the developing countries, it is clear that this poverty is very widespread and has reached an extreme degree in those countries where the poorest part of the population, which is estimated at between 920 million and 1200 million inhabitants, is living in a state bordering on absolute destitution.

Per capita income and natural income are, by themselves, inadequate indicators for measuring the gap which separates the rich nations from the others. Therefore, any estimate of relative advantages and disadvantages must go beyond the notion of total or average income and embrace the real distribution of income between social classes. In this way it becomes possible to take account of other indicators such as birth rates and death rates, the level of literacy and education, life expectancy, the availability of natural resources, and, lastly, access to the commercial markets of other countries. For example, even if Algeria's receipts from oil increased its *per capita* income to $710 in 1974, that country's authorities are still disturbed by its infant mortality rate, which continues to be high (126 deaths of children less than one year old per 1000 live births).

Similarly, although India and Sri Lanka have practically the same *per capita* incomes ($140 for the former and $130 for the latter), the two countries differ markedly when their rates of infant mortality, literacy and life expectancy are compared. These differences can be seen in the index of the physical quality of life. For Sri Lanka, for example, it is 83, while for India it is 41.

We also find that, although the total number of inhabitants of the developing countries who do not know how to read or write increased from 701 million in 1960 to 756 million in 1970, in reality there has been a decline in the percentage of illiterates, since it dropped from 59 per cent in 1960 to 50 per cent in 1970. In spite of this over-all improvement, illiteracy is still a major problem for women. In 1970, approximately 60 per cent of all women (as opposed to 40 per cent of men) in the developing countries did not know how to read and write.

Endogenous development and exchanges
with the outside world

What is basically needed in order to remedy such a disturbing social situation is an *endogenous* development, which calls for a new structure of internal production—a reorientation of the choice of industries—and a new social policy—a reorganization of services.

This does not exclude exchanges with the outside world, but the latter should constitute a planned, i.e. controlled, complement to the strategy of endogenous development.

Even though it ignores the inevitable inequality of such exchanges— deterioration of the terms of trade, extroversion of production, inadequate exploitation of raw materials at the source—foreign trade does constitute a more important component for the development prospects of the poor nations than aid or even investment.

It is necessary to stress the noticeable differences between these countries, and between these countries and the industrialized countries, with regard to the amount of foreign currency they have available, thanks to their natural resources and their different export capacities.

In 1975, as shown in Appendix II, the total exports of the developed market economies were estimated at $580,500 million, representing 66 per cent of the value of world exports. On the other hand, the exports of the developing market economies for the same year amounted to $211,200 million, or only 24 per cent of the world total; the OPEC countries alone accounted for more than half ($113,900 million) of the total value of the exports of the developing countries.

It is not without interest to note that the trade patterns are different according to groups of countries. Although the developed market economies supply 38 per cent of world exports of raw materials (including fuels), these products represent only 24 per cent of the total value of their exports; manufactured goods make up nearly 75 per cent of the exports of the market economies of the industrialized countries and 57 per cent of those of the centrally planned economies. On the other hand, nearly 83 per cent of the exports of the developing market economies consists of raw materials, while manufactured articles constitute the largest part of their imports.

If we view this general situation—unsatisfied social needs, unequal terms of trade—against the daily reality of each country and group of countries, a micro-analysis will give us a better idea, for example, of the population in question, its growth rate, its internal and external migrations, its occupational structure and employment index, its division into social classes and income levels. Such analysis will help us to determine certain measurable aspects like the biological, technical, educational, housing, cultural and even civic levels.

After all, by viewing a population in its own environment (physical structure of the country, quality of the soil, weather, agrarian patterns, etc.), we can understand the local conditions of development without which no progress is possible. "Human beings rise", says Lebret, "from the foundations which are already there." The elements revealed by this illuminating approach enable us to identify the factors of imbalance—historical, geographic, technical, economic and political—all of which represent so many handicaps to be overcome. To give one example: in several countries of the Third World, even the poorest, military expenditures are proportionately greater than those for education and health. All of us are participating collectively in this universal wastage, as a result of which, every *hour* of every *day*, $35 million are being spent for armies, which added up to $300,000 million annually, in 1975, whereas many experts agree that only $15,000 million, or twenty times less, would be sufficient to meet the most urgent basic needs during the next 10 years.

What is still worse, the frantic arms race is creating a constantly growing demand for various raw materials, such as bauxite, copper, iron, lead, manganese, petroleum and rare metals, most of which come from the Third World. The countries which depend on this situation for their resources naturally want it to continue. This is precisely the tragic aspect of our time, which Perroux has described as the agonizing tryptych of population, arms, subsistence.

Basic needs and a regime of strict economy

This example gives us a better idea of the importance of the factors of imbalance and the value of a strategy of development based on basic needs.

In 1969, Mr. David Morse, who had just appointed me Assistant-

Director General of the International Labour Office, made me responsible, among other things, for supervising the Conditions of Work and Life Department. This enabled me to take part in a very interesting experiment which was closely connected with the strategy of priority needs.

We had to organize several field surveys in Latin America and Asia with a view to determining, in the first place, the main objectives which really met the aspirations of the people of the countries involved. In the framework of this survey, one of my assistants undertook to question the people concerned directly (peasants, housewives, young people, trade union members, etc.) and to compare their replies with those of the persons responsible for administering the Plan in the capitals of the countries concerned.

Although the details about the survey have been kept confidential, the conclusions reached in this study were that the planners in the capital often had their eyes fixed on national accounting, the balance of trade and productivity which were subject to organized pressure within the country and abroad by more or less powerful groups . . . , whereas, on the other hand, the replies given by the peasants and certain categories of workers in the cities clearly suggested another approach, which I shall sum up as follows:

1. The need for everybody to *work* in an intelligent and well-organized way to increase the production of essential goods and services within the framework of controlled economic growth.

2. Priority to be given to a definite improvement of the people's living conditions over a specific period in development plans.

3. The need to create jobs in order to give the majority of the population the practical means for satisfying their needs.

4. The need to organize and integrate economic activities so as to bring about a more equitable distribution of income.

The strategy as summed up above was the same as that which has received general approval in various public discussions and which found particular favour at the World Employment Conference in 1976: that first priority should be given to meeting the basic needs of the individual as well as of the community.[8] And here I should like to

---

[8] See in particular Francis Blanchard (Director General of the International Labour Office), *Employment, Growth and Basic Needs, Report to the Tripartite World Conference on Employment* (Geneva, 1976).

emphasize, as I already pointed out at the beginning of this book, that, to my way of thinking, the "satisfaction of *basic* needs" amounts to the same thing as the "social *control* of needs".

This strategy is directly aimed at all sectors of the population, and more particularly at individuals and groups whose income is below the bare minimum.

The work to be done in order to achieve these objectives also takes place at various levels. It involves mainly changing the way in which productive resources are used, as well as the type of growth:

—by large investments in the production of goods and services which are more labour-intensive;

—by introducing suitable techniques for increasing the productivity of all workers, including those most in need;

—by the increased utilization of local natural resources for useful production.

The distribution of income will immediately be improved, provided that the planners make proposals that will lead the way to:

(a) giving suitable vocational training to the greatest number of people;

(b) ensuring a more equitable distribution of land ownership and opportunities for access to land.

All this presupposes institutional reforms which will enable the population to participate more effectively in major decisions and ensure State support for structural reforms.

Knowing how much such a strategy depends on world economic trends, we can better understand the need for establishing new international relations and creating closer co-operation between countries of the Third World.

If our aim is to satisfy everybody's basic needs by everybody's efforts to utilize the earth's resources, which belong to everybody, I can see only one policy for attaining this goal, that which the Chinese have called the *regime of strict economy*, based on a self-reliant form of collective development, to which three criteria apply: to rely on one's own forces, on one's own resources and on the creative capacities of one's people.

The "regime of strict economy" is not an austerity plan along the lines of an emergency policy which calls for occasional and involuntary sacrifices. On the contrary, the regime of strict economy should be designed, formulated and applied on a long-term basis.

Mao Tse-tung himself described it for the first time in the speech he delivered at the eleventh session of the Supreme State Conference on 27 February 1957:

"We want to carry out a large-scale building plan, but our country is still very poor—that involves a contradiction. One of the means to solve it is to make sustained efforts towards applying a regime of strict economy covering all fields. It is necessary to create more enterprises, both small and medium-sized, to work as economically as possible, to do more with less money, to combat waste in every aspect of the life of the country."

That is a simple and coherent policy. Because it is simple and coherent, it is a difficult one if people have become accustomed to not knowing how to live on little, to begging and letting things go to waste, to not being able to imagine any other models or other practices.

The African cosmogonies represent life as a cycle in which all living beings depend on one another. The higher you go in the hierarchy of species, the greater becomes their vital inter-dependence. This inter-dependence might be represented by a pyramid, the base of which would be the vegetable kingdom, which in turn supports the animal species, while man is the apex of the edifice.

Our priority goal, the satisfaction of basic human needs, cannot be attained in a self-reliant model of development unless, like the biological pyramid, the social edifice rests on a broad foundation formed by a vigorous rural sector that has not been oppressed.

Better nutrition from agriculture

In general, when reference is made to the advancement of the rural world, it is in terms of its capacity for greater production and not in terms of human wealth and the development of the peasants themselves. As I have already pointed out, the official economic goals and the social goals at the base are often incompatible.

From now on, we will have to reconcile the two. "Doing more things with less money" will involve making better use of existing resources, increasing and diversifying production, reducing losses in harvesting, transport and the preservation of foodstuffs.

At the village level—or at least that of a group of related villages— an effort should be made to cultivate all the products which are necessary for a balanced diet, with a view to the maximum of self-sufficiency subject, of course, to the condition that the crops are well adapted to the soil and that constant care is taken to protect the eco-system and to restore the biological balance of the earth itself. Since people will only settle in places where they find means of subsistence, areas which are overworked and irreparably exhausted will in any case be abandoned.

It is not a matter of decreeing that everybody has to eat the same food. However, the economists and nutritionists who might be called upon to determine the minimum to be supplied would be under a strict obligation to take account of the ecological environment and the traditions of the community in question.

A few weeks before his death, Josué de Castro, who had just founded the Centre International pour le Développement (International Centre for Development) in Paris, had a conversation with me which I venture to describe as one of fundamental importance.

"If you are one day called upon to diagnose the degree of develop-ment of a non-industrialized country", he told me, "make it your business to find out about the diet of the Prime Minister or the Head of State.

"If the chief cook in the Government palace is a foreigner—and a European to boot—you can already draw a tentative conclusion about the degree of confidence placed in the culinary skills of the women of that country or of all those who may be able to carry out properly such important and significant duties. . . . Moreover, if the menus are drawn up in the style of Malossol caviar on toast Melba, *velouté Victor Hugo*, *Aiglefin aux câpres*, *filet de boeuf Wellington*, and if the national dishes are only served as an amusement, a weekend fantasy, then you can tremble for your mission. You will, in fact, have reason to fear that the country is launched on a road to development which is not designed to favour either its local resources or the basic needs of its people. For, from the President's table down to that of his servants, and from them down to their families and friends, the tendency will be to prefer an 'aristocratic' diet. Everyone will want from time to time to do as the President's boy does in the market-place. And so one day there will be crowds of people in front of the bakeries trying to get a bit of wheaten bread. . . .

"On the other hand", Josué de Castro went on, "if preference is given to yams rather than to potatoes at the President's table, even when he entertains distinguished foreigners, if proper consideration is given to maize, millet, cassava and cowpeas, then you can be sure that full use is being made of local resources and that the peasant has some chance of participating in a development plan which really involves him."

This is what the distinguished author of *The Geopolitics of Hunger* told me in the modest apartment in Paris where he had to end his days. I had the feeling at the time that what I heard was a veritable testament which I could not keep for myself alone. And as an indication of the truth of his remarks, I should like to say that among the many documents I receive every day about the Third World, its people and its problems, I recently noticed one highly instructive booklet. Its title is: *Cowpeas: Home Preparation and Use in West Africa*. The authors are three young African women from Nigeria and Sierra Leone: Florence Dovlo, Caroline Williams and Laraba Zoaka, whose study was supported by the International Development Research Centre in Ottawa.[9]

This study shows us that the cowpea (also called the niébé, red bean, dolic de Chine), which is cultivated in almost all African countries, is a very nutritious and inexpensive vegetable, which is capable of supplying a large proportion of the proteins needed for good health.

The cultivation of the cowpea almost certainly originated in Africa, and in 1972 Africa was producing 94 per cent of the world crop, mainly in Nigeria, Upper Volta, Uganda, Niger, Senegal and Tanzania. This vegetable is widely used, not only in the countryside but also in the cities, where it is always so reasonably priced that it is helpful to many housewives when drought, inflation and the decline in purchasing

[9] Ottawa, International Development Research Centre, 1976. I should also like to draw attention to the excellent little book written by Jean and Rose Pliya: *Alimentation de santé en Afrique traditionnelle—avec menus et recettes naturistes africains* (Paris, Editions of the review *Vivre en harmonie*, 1974).

power of workers' incomes make food scarce or expensive. In addition, it can be prepared in many different ways. For example, the preparation of *akara* balls, made with cowpeas, is a widespread local industry throughout West Africa. Since women have a monopoly of it, this guarantees them employment in the rural, village and urban communities. If I place particular emphasis on this quality product, it is because the cowpea has a protein content of 20 to 25 per cent, or double that of most cereals, and its nutritive value is increased still further by the African custom of mixing it with various products in the same dish (rice and cowpeas, cowpeas and maize, etc.).[10]

Protein insufficiency is serious everywhere in the developing countries. Some people claim that the best way to remedy this deficiency would be to increase shipments of cattle, fish meal, eggs or milk from the industrialized countries or from international organizations. But such a solution would only perpetuate our dependence and the bad habit of begging: whereas in many African countries the cowpea represents a start towards a solution, especially since research in its production, such as that which has been carried out since 1970 under the Programme for the Improvement of Seed Vegetables of the International Institute of Tropical Agriculture in Ibadan (Nigeria), shows encouraging prospects for the development of varieties of high-yield cowpeas.

Compared with a present average of 360 kilos per hectare in West Africa, it is possible to obtain yields of 1000 kilos per hectare in favourable conditions in semi-arid areas, and even yields of 2500 to 2900 kilos per hectare at research centres.

Another example in the same field: while orange trees grow easily in a certain temperate Andean area, they are generally neglected, the fruit is left to rot and is not eaten. Yet citrus fruits would constitute a valuable source of vitamin C, which is lacking in a diet consisting mainly of starchy foods.

These examples taken from the field of nutrition enable us to picture an economy based on the full utilization of local resources, using a simple technology directly accessible to those concerned.

---

[10] The table opposite, published in the booklet by Dovlo, Williams and Zoaka (p. 12), gives the nutritional values of cowpeas and other foodstuffs found in Africa.

Nutritional value of cowpeas and a few other foods

(Platt, B. Table of Representative Values of Foods Commonly Used in Tropical Countries. N.p., Medical Research Corps, 1962.)

	Cal/100g	Protein (%)	Fat (%)	Carbo-hydrate (%)	Vitamin A (I.U./100g)	Thiamin (mg/100g)	Ribo-flavin (mg/100g)	Nicotinic acid (mg/100g)	Ascorbic acid (mg/100g)
Cowpeas	340	22.0	1.5	60	20	0.90	0.15	2.0	0
Candle millet (flour)	332	5.5	0.8	76	0	0.15	0.07	0.8	0
Maize (flour) 96% extr.	362	9.5	4.0	72	0[a]	0.30	0.13	1.5	0
Rice (slightly ground)	354	8.0	1.5	77	0	0.25	0.05	2.0	0
Sorghum (flour)	353	10.0	2.5	73	0	0.40	0.10	3.0	0
Cassava (flour)	153	0.7	0.2	37	0	0.07	0.03	0.7	0
Yams (fresh)	104	2.0	0.2	24	20	0.10	0.03	0.4	30
Bambarra, peanuts (fresh)	367	18.0	6.0	60	0	0.30	0.10	2.0	10
Peanuts (dried)	579	27.0	45.0	17	0	0.90	0.15	17.0	0
Soya	382	35.0	18.0	20	0	1.10	0.30	2.0	0
Sea fish (lean fillet)	73	17.0	0.5	0	0	0.05	0.10	2.5	0
Beef (lean)	202	19.0	14.0	0	0	0.10	0.20	5.0	0
Eggs (hen)	158	13.0	11.5	0.5	1000	0.12	0.35	0.1	0

[a] Yellow maize, 150 I.U. (International Units) (Stanton, W. Grain Legumes in Africa. Rome, FAO, 1964).

The need to develop village technology

This "simple village technology" has, in fact, a vital rôle to play. Its advantage is "to make maximum use of *cheap* materials which are familiar to the largest possible number of people and available to them"[11] and, let us add, often better suited to them.

To achieve the benefits of a simple technology for 2500 million persons, which is the population of the Third World now living in villages, raises a great number of problems. But it is in any case worth trying, especially if we are trying to achieve strict economy together with the participation of peoples in their own development plan for the kind of society they want.

For example, there are some areas where the lack of electricity immediately rules out any use of sophisticated tools; on the other hand, there is undoubtedly some technical knowledge in those places which has been neglected or has fallen into disuse under the impact of "modernization" and which could be usefully revived. Clay, water and a stand are all that are needed to make pottery for a number of different uses. There are thousands of places where calabashes are more practical than many imported utensils. UNICEF, FAO and a number of public and private organizations, together with research workers all over the world, are studying these traditional techniques which can bring to village dwellers simple technologies for many practical uses—such as better methods of cooking, grinding, milling and husking cereal grains and oil seeds, dehydrating plants for the more efficient storage of different crops, installing or improving water-supply systems, harnessing wind and water power for pumping water and for other uses.

Peasant societies often have a very intelligent sense of how to adapt their habitat to space and climate; man is as one with his environment, he does not "lose contact" with the natural elements of the region but rather makes use of them as fully as possible to obtain effective protection. The traditional techniques of housing construction in Casamance, for example, make it possible to maintain a distinct difference of temperature *in the shade* between the inside and outside of a house.

[11] Alan Robinson, head of the Food and Technological Section of UNICEF.

Other ingenious examples of peasant architecture are to be found on all continents: cave villages in Mali, Tuareg tents, houses on pilings in the rice-growing regions of Asia, reed villages on floating islands on Lake Titicaca. Everywhere man has found some particular response to the challenges of his surroundings. However, almost everywhere, unfortunately, the traditional materials are being replaced by imported materials.

A sheet metal roof is becoming a mark of prestige in Africa. But the sheet metal turns the dwelling into an oven under the sun or into a sound-box under the rain.

While using local materials and natural power sources is without doubt economical in itself, waste can also be avoided by reusing and recycling products.

Waste materials can be used for feeding domestic animals, but they can also be a useful natural fertilizer, free of charge, for manuring the fields or can also be transformed into methane.

"The manufacture of methane is well adapted to small farms: one hectare of cereals could yield a quantity of methane equivalent to 560 litres of petrol", Laurent Samuel and Dominique Simonnet assure us.[12]

In the field of health, we have at last realized that it is possible to improve living conditions without always calling upon modern medical science, which is extremely costly and often of more mythical than real value.

Staying healthy, as we know, is first of all a matter of knowing how to meet attacks on one's health by one's own efforts. Western medicine is now studying the practices of traditional methods of medicine. Every culture, in fact, has hidden treasures waiting to be rediscovered and put to use. Chinese acupuncture is the best known example. In India, modern medicine is finding support in an ancient Hindu practice, ayurveda or the "Science of life", which has existed for perhaps 3000 years. This system of medicine takes account of the psychosomatic constitution of the patient; it lays stress on measures of personal and social hygiene and advocates physical exercises,

---

[12] *L'homme et son environnement* (Paris, Editions Retz, 1976), p. 470.

medicinal herbs and natural elements.[13] India now has 400,000 ayurvedic practitioners, most of whom practise in rural areas, where they are very close to the people.

At the neuro-psychiatric centre of Dakar, Professor Coulomb treats his patients with reference to the social and family conditions in which they suffered the shock to their nervous system. The film "Kodou" produced by the Senegalese B. Samb, provides a good illustration of this therapy, which is essentially African.

It is of paramount importance that the population should take an active part in its own medical service.

But it is not enough for even a simple technology to be effective; it must also set people free. What I mean by this is a technique which is not imposed from the outside but sought for and accepted by the people and even created by them and thus integrated into the practice of a group having a definite objective. Such a technique is creative of wealth. It is, as we now say, "convivial", because it is "radical"— i.e. of a "grass-roots" nature.[14]

The inventive spirit, the creativity of individuals, ought to be encouraged at all levels. If a certain kind of canary-filter has been invented in one village, for example, that does not mean that other solutions cannot be found elsewhere. The important thing is to respect each group's autonomy. The choice of a society based on self-reliance means that priority should be given to the use of a technology which is integrated in social reality and aimed at a real inter-connection between man and the biosphere. Although it makes use of simple means, such a technology is far from being poor; on the contrary, it creates a richness in the heart of the social organism, the richness of the biological relation between man and the natural elements, the richness of the feeling of belonging to some place on earth, the awareness of having

---

[13] H. Breetveld in *News from UNICEF*, No. 87, 1976, "The Right to Health".

[14] For Valentina Borremans, the main criterion for a "radical" technology lies in the possibilities it creates for individuals or small groups to produce objects of use value and thus to free themselves from the need engendered by mercantile consumer goods. To pursue this line of thought further, see: Project for a "Guide to Use-value oriented Convivial Tools and their Enemies"—Borremans, Valentina, Tecno Política Doc. 77/6, Cuernavaca, Mexico, August 1977.

a fatherland, the awareness of belonging to a human and social universe, and lastly, the richness of rediscovering time to live.

Murray Brooklin explains this wealth which is acquired by the "liberating" technology as follows: "to bring back the sun, the wind, the earth—in fact the *foundations of life*—into technology, into the processes used by man for his survival, would reactivate the ties between man and nature in a revolutionary way. To re-establish this dependence in such a way that every human group would become aware, through it, of the singularity of every region, that it would become aware not only of its dependence on nature in general but also of the way in which this dependence is specifically manifested in a certain region possessing a certain quality would give this act of renewal a genuinely ecological character. We would see the formation of a genuinely ecological system, a network delicately woven of local riches, constantly receiving aids from science and art. In proportion as a genuine sense of locality was developed, each resource would find its place in a stable equilibrium, an organic blend of natural, social and technological elements."

In a regime of strict economy, in fact, the prior accumulation of capital would no longer be a decisive factor in the development of productive forces. "Living work is the factor which is directly and immediately decisive and dominant, whereas dead work is only a subordinate and secondary factor." One of the reasons why I was so strongly impressed by my brief trip to China in 1976 was the extraordinary proliferation of small and medium-sized industrial enterprises, which, according to observers, have "grown like mushrooms" in the countryside. This example shows that it is possible to follow a different road towards industrialization from that which consists in building large production units of the capitalist type, and to break away from the opposition between the industrial cities and rural areas devoted to agriculture alone.[15]

---

[15] The reader interested in these matters will undoubtedly wish to refer to the recent book by Denis Goulet: *The Uncertain Promise—Value Conflicts in Technology Transfer*, published in 1977 in collaboration with the Overseas Development Council, Washington; see in particular chapter 7, "Development Strategies: Basic Options".

Industrial self-reliance in the service of agriculture

A country which relies on its own natural and human resources is able to make full use of its entire economic potential. During their Congress in Algiers, the economists of the Third World very rightly questioned the international division of labour. They felt that, rather than being forced to sell their primary products, it is better to exploit them on the spot for the country's own needs.

If the level of living of the rural majority of the population rises, the internal market will expand and industry will find sales outlets. *Agricultural development alone can support a genuine industrial development.* There are three reasons for this: the purchasing power of the population will increase; agriculture will supply industry with raw materials; and industry will supply agriculture with the goods it needs. Timber, vegetable fibres and leather will be processed to supply the people with clothing and other articles of primary necessity. Light industries will be developed to produce goods for every-day consumption.

Even if simple techniques and local materials are used in the agricultural sector, it will still be necessary to resort to heavy industry in order to develop adequate and profitable production. This may be needed for building dams, irrigating an area, or using mechanical equipment. In a country where the staple food of the people is rice and the national production of rice is too low, there are three possible solutions: to import rice from abroad, to import fertilizers to increase production, or to produce the necessary fertilizers on the spot. This last solution is the best. From the point of view of medium-term planning, it is perhaps more economical to set up a chemical industry at home if the resources and size of the country so permit.

In this way, industry supported by agriculture would constitute the second widest tier in the pyramid, while there would be a whole network of exchanges and reciprocal services between the two sectors.

In a regime of strict economy, the development of the secondary sector presents three main challenges, three kinds of choice for a society which aims at poverty for each individual and wealth for all. How can we make the best possible use of the three factors in production: technology, investment and labour?

Striking a balance between light and heavy industry

Although at this point I cannot deal with the vast problem of the conditions, means and stages of industrialization of each of the countries, in relation to their resources and their size, I should like to draw attention to two mistakes which continue to be the source of many failures. One is to try to proceed too quickly while ignoring realities; the other is to be satisfied with encouraging a few small industrial activities chosen haphazardly from suggestions coming from anywhere.

In November 1972, I was lucky enough to participate in the International Seminar on African Industrial Development, organized in Dakar jointly by the Government of Senegal and the European Centre for Overseas Industrial Equipment and Development (CEDIMOM). This seminar was particularly interesting and successful—because, among other things, participants with widely divergent views were able to express them freely since the purpose of the meeting was to try to reconcile positions such as that of Thierry Mieg, Director of the French Niger Company (UNILEVER), and the points of view of Morad Castel, Secretary General of the Ministry of Industry in Algeria.

For my part, I stirred up a row—quite unwittingly—at that meeting by taking a vigorous stand against certain proposals for a kind of industrial giantism in which I did not believe at all, and even today I continue to stress the need to observe phases and rates of growth in accordance with the following criteria:

—We must not impair the internal production and consumption of foodstuffs.

—We must know how to use and integrate techniques which are either already known or easily learned.

—We must depend on foreign countries as little as possible for investments and the importation of technology.

—We must observe the proper order of phases for gradual integration of internal economic activities.

Since we are at a similar stage of development, we may possibly profit from experiments carried out in some of the smaller countries in Asia with industrial enterprises of very modest dimensions, which supply the essential goods needed for food, clothing and housing made from local materials.

Preference should therefore be given to small or medium-sized industries which make use of local resources for local needs. They play an important part in creating use values and increasing employment. In this capacity, they ought to constitute the main substance of the industrial sector.

At the same time, however, larger units are needed for certain kinds of activities, especially those which are at the source of other forms of production; it is impossible to ignore heavy industry altogether.

The important point is that we must keep a very close watch on the means used to establish this sector, since, directly or indirectly, they may run counter to the very goals assigned to it: to develop a self-reliant form of industrialization and an egalitarian incomes structure.

After all, heavy industry requires very expensive techniques which the industrialized countries alone possess at the present time. Whether we appeal to foreign aid, loans or multinational firms, the result is that we become more or less strongly dependent on the outside world. This kind of industry provides few jobs and calls for a sufficiently large national market to support it as well as the means of developing the subsidiary industries to which normally it would give rise. China, India and Brazil can already offer a technical threshold and economies of scale of this kind, but many of the States of the Third World are not very large. Steel mills, for example, would not be profitable in West Africa except at the supranational level within a pan-African framework of industrialization involving the implantation of complementary industries at the regional level.

When I held the office of Secretary General of the African and Malagasy Union from 1961 to 1963, our major difficulty was to persuade the partners in the Union to take advantage of it to organize a production and consumption area which would really make sense. It was evident that the small-scale developments that everyone was anxious to make the most profit from could not provide the basis for efficient industrialization. More than once, in private conversations and on public occasions, I tried to put over the following argument.[16]

Taking a sensible realistic approach, let us consider our countries as they actually are, with their geographical limits, which may seem artificial but are becoming more and more real, with their many different languages and their great diversity in every field. But let us also acknowledge an even more stubborn fact. Faced with the gigantic resources and achievements of countries such as the United States of America or the Soviet Union, faced with the patiently organized labour of 800 million Chinese, confronted with the steadily increasing economic power of the European Common Market, and at a time when men are extending the horizons of power by their conquests in space—if, in these circumstances, the African countries were called upon to remain confined to a narrow nationalism, responsible only for administering the diminishing market of raw materials, some of which are becoming less and less necessary because of the increasing use of synthetics, and if they were unable to realize the need for getting together and organizing themselves, the inevitable result would be that not only would the gap between the rich and poor countries widen, but also that the whole continent might find itself pushed out on the fringe and condemned to the role of a mere dependency of some empire—old and new.

Even if the unification of the countries concerned in one large territory was an impossible dream, it seemed to me at the time that a genuine confederation was still possible. Instead of which we keep dragging along in this "balkanization" which is like a broken mirror and which, as Sartre would say ("The Frogs who asked for a King"), offers the spectacle of a continent which is "compartmentalized, bristling with barriers, walls and traps, where they are all fighting with each other over a bare bone".[17]

---

[16] See Albert Tévoédjrè: *Pan-Africanism in Action: An Account of the UAM,* Harvard University Center for International Affairs, 1965; see also Albert Ekué: *L'Union africaine et malgache,* doctoral thesis for the Faculté des Lettres of the University of Bordeaux, 1976.

[17] This is so true that at every threat of economic disaster we witness arbitrary and large-scale expulsions of whole tribes of "foreigners"—their property stolen or confiscated in defiance of the laws of humanity—cruelty being pushed to a point where pregnant women, babies and old people who only want to be allowed to rest in peace are driven across frontiers—which have been falsely baptized as "national" frontiers. And we talk about "human and fraternal" Africa!

It still seems to me that what Kwame Nkrumah then called the geopolitical outlook must come about not through direct or disguised annexations but through voluntary co-operation. For what was needed at that time and what is still needed is to seek after *workable relations*, to bear in mind and to translate into reality, as Hegel[18] taught, that the whole is true, only the whole is real, that a large territory cultivated by a sufficient number of willing arms and minds that can act as producers as well as consumers remains one of the major keys to development.

Failing that, costs will always be too high and the setbacks with which we are all more or less familiar will make it necessary to sacrifice production for immediate needs and basic popular consumption.

This emphasizes the need to strike a balance, according to sectors of activity and types of product, between, on the one hand, the small- and medium-sized industries established by local communities and, on the other, the large or heavy industry which in some conditions calls for regional integration.

Restoring the value of work
Developing the non-organized productive sector

However, regardless of the size of the units, we must be careful to ensure that the production process is controlled by the workers themselves. The technical problems which inevitably arise can generally be solved by the workers inside the factory, provided they have made the enterprise into their own instrument of production and participate in its management. The most important wealth, as I have already said, is certainly not the financial capital we own, but our human ability to work, to plan and to innovate.

Here I shall again refer to China, although I recognize that this country, like every society, is undoubtedly suffering from its own contradictions and from limitations which the daily news sometimes brings to our attention.[19]

[18] See Hegel: *Ecrits politiques*, in particular the essay "La Constitution de l'Allemagne" (Paris, Editions Champ libre, 1977).

[19] See Aubert, C. and others: *Regards froids sur la Chine* (Paris, Éditions du Seuil, 1976).

In the general knitted goods factory in Peking, a worker points out that "the goals of this technical revolution are proposed by the different workshops, with a view to improving quality, raising labour productivity, guaranteeing safety and reducing working tension. It is generally in these areas that technical innovations are made. In this way we will be able to discover new raw materials, new techniques, new technologies, new equipment and new methods. We are always looking for the techniques that offer the most advantages and cause the least waste. Technical innovations are a very important means of developing industry."[20]

The same worker emphasizes that "it is worth-while to take two or even five years to create a good plant. The most important thing is for the workers to be mobilized and that they find out for themselves where innovation is needed, for it is up to the working class to liberate itself."

Apart from investment in labour, local savings constitute the most important part in the accumulation of capital. *Taxes* already represent a form of forced savings which should be used to a greater extent for productive investments. It is only too easy to say that there is but small capacity for savings in the Third World. If all the capital exported by the rich classes were invested in the country and if imports of non-essential products were eliminated, it would be possible to recover substantial sums with which to develop the productive sector. Low production and poverty are largely due to the inroads made by privileged individuals. In most cases, the national wealth, if better used and better distributed, would be sufficient to enable national savings to provide the driving force in a gradually widening economic circuit, especially if another category of enterprises, that of the "marginal jobs" in the "non-structured urban sector", were included in the circuit of a self-reliant economy.

In fact, the multitude of small trades which form a part of daily life in the cities, the innumerable small shops of miscellaneous craftsmen, such as tailors, shoemakers, etc. and even certain itinerant tradesmen, constitute a very flexible and highly diversified network, the value of which should be acknowledged. To be sure, due to the lack of

---

[20] Charles Bettelheim: *Révolution culturelle et organisation industrielle en Chine* (Paris, Maspero, 1973, p. 26).

productive jobs, a whole parasitical trade has often developed which constitutes an important inflationary factor in times of scarcity. However, there are many basic activities which provide services and simple products which are in demand by the majority of the population and which therefore count for something in the national economy, although they are poorly defined and only too often ignored.

The small enterprises to which I refer play an important role in the life of the country. They should be made an essential sector because they offer substantial economies and are designed by poor people for poor people. Their actual and potential riches are obvious; in various respects they are much more advantageous than enterprises of the modern "structured sector" in the cities. They use very little capital and a lot of human resources. The spirit of enterprise, a sense of organization and innovation are often to be found among these numerous and resourceful workers.

This sector is also very important in creating income and providing a livelihood for a large proportion of the urban population: it provides 24 to 30 per cent of all jobs in the cities of Kenya, more than 30 per cent of employment in Abidjan, 25 per cent in Calcutta and more than 40 per cent in Djakarta. The handicrafts and commercial activities of the poor people in the cities are based solely on local resources; vocational skills are acquired "on the job" and trading is largely open to competition. This kind of enterprise operates on a small scale and is satisfied with modest receipts. Accordingly, they attract innumerable customers among the poor and mobilize for productive purposes savings which are spread throughout the largest classes of the population.

Today, these marginal, small-scale activities are supplementing the economy of the modern sector, which profits by them and sometimes exploits them. The small eating places crowding around the factories allow the latter's managers to avoid installing canteens or factory restaurants. In districts where trucks cannot enter, deliveries are made by hand-carts or rickshaws. In places where no enterprise is willing to take the trouble, repairs are nevertheless carried out on bicycles and various machines.

This non-structured sector deserves to be protected so that it can become better organized and integrated into the economy, and thus take its place as an essential, dynamic sector and a decisive factor for national development.

Small enterprises can be encouraged and helped to overcome the weaknesses due to their small size by the offer of loans and the means to train their employees, improve their techniques and manage the various aspects of their business more efficiently.[21] If developed and supported in this way, this sector would gradually make possible a more efficient integration of the modern sector in the national economy. A complex network of subcontractors was one of the characteristics of the Japanese economy when it was taking off. Above all, however, these small enterprises are perfectly adapted to the local scale, that of everyday life, whether in the village or the urban quarter.

In that way we would have a new spatial distribution of productive forces, which would no longer be centred around increasingly extensive and overpowering cities. Then there might be a start towards a movement away from the cities. Collective life would be enriched by an urban area designed for pedestrians rather than automobiles.

This would, of course, require the improvement of communication routes and the construction of new ones so that no community would be left isolated. The example may be cited of the construction of the Tanzania-Zambia railway, which defied the customary rules of international co-operation, according to which it would have been impossible. Actually, however, the Tazara was not designed solely for economic

[21] It is in connection with the non-structured sector, in fact, that there has been talk about "barefoot management". Michael v.d. Bogaert, Director of the Xavier Institute of Social Service at Bihar, in India, devoted a very interesting article to this subject: "Barefooted Management for Social Change" in *Impact* (Manila), Vol. 11, No. 8, August 1976, p. 270. This article states that "one of the greatest benefits of barefoot management would be the liberation of the concept of management". From being tied up with business enterprise, a privileged class or a particular socio-economic system (the free-market system), management would become universalized. E. H. McGrath goes so far as to advocate management for everyone: "Management is a practice, specifically and pre-eminently human, which is required by all people, in any organization, under any socio-political system. Management can even be used to change social systems and social relations. However poorly we may do it, we are all managing. We plan and set goals, use information, we decide and implement, we define and solve problems. We evaluate. We are all engaged in the execution of desired goals through the direction of human energies and resources." McGrath therefore advocates that "management training based on work experience should form an integral and essential part of every man, woman and child's education, or in other words, management training is for everyone".

reasons, nor solely to enable Zambia to export and Tanzania to exploit its mines in the South. It was also built in order to revive and rescue from isolation areas spread out over a distance of nearly 1000 kilometres which had been completely abandoned or which had no links to any country or to any neighbour. Today, they have advanced to a life which may not be modern but which is a modernized village life, in other words, a life in which basic needs are beginning to be met.

Against bureaucracy—giving free creativity a chance

One way of economizing on resources would be to cut down the administrative paperwork for the benefit of these villagers who have just emerged from their isolation, by simplifying formalities. Bureaucratic hypertrophy is not only a "disease" in the countries of the Third World, but this veritable gangrene is at its most dangerous among them when it reaches the heights of absurdity: for example, when certificates, visas and stamps are needed at every police station, when entering every community, in order to travel a distance of 50 kilometres. In this connection, the tribulations undergone by one of the heroes of Sembène Ousmane in order to cash a money order are highly significant; likewise waiting for several months in order to obtain the card required for getting a job, for re-entering or leaving the country and so forth.

While every person of common sense would agree that one of the first tasks of a good administration is to identify its citizens, international reports, which are sometimes of a confidential nature, indicate that in some countries the issuance of an ordinary identity card can become a real problem. And this situation is welcomed by thieves and other dubious characters for whom anonymity is the supreme blessing.

The administration creates jobs, but they are not directly productive jobs and are sometimes of a parasitical nature. The white collar myth impoverishes those who believe in it and who often try to gain power over others by petty annoyances or by squeezing money out of them.

If all those who are crowded for no good purpose into costly office buildings were reassigned to jobs which are really useful to the community, this would represent a tremendous economic gain and social progress.

Such an effort would, of course, call for material sacrifices by those who occupy privileged positions in the existing system. Money would have to be "dethroned" in favour of a better supply of collective goods and services.

What is needed most for achieving such a result is the participation of the largest possible number of workers rather than maximum productivity calculated in economic terms. Leisure time and non-profit-making activities are also valuable goods, as well as a fundamental right.

Besides indispensable productive work, it is conceivable that the leisure time allowed to people might also be used to produce "useless" things simply because they are pleasing, beautiful or even—why not?—harmless. As soon as one takes account of social costs and benefits, words change their meaning: one could then speak of the "production of social relations" or the "production of beauty". The accumulative criterion would then no longer be the sole judge; human activities would no longer then be reduced to their mere market value and their end-benefit to the productive system. Today, the obligation to produce as an end in itself is destroying many of man's other values. These are the values we have to rediscover.

Sometimes when talking about Africans it is said that they are oil men or cotton men. Senghor replies, "We are the dancing men whose feet regain vigour by pounding the hard earth." This reply shows the richness of life as opposed to those who are unwilling to see in man anything but an economic factor, an element of commercial production.

A regime of convivial frugality based on a self-reliant collective development, which mobilizes the energies of peoples involved in the creation of their own future, and is aimed at satisfying the basic needs of a society united by a common feeling of solidarity—this I believe to be the foundation of a new kind of economy.

Statistics and research in the service of welfare

This other kind of economy is not solely quantitative since everything in it cannot be measured. (It was Pareto who warned us that "the importance of facts counts for more than their number; a single fact which is well observed and well described is worth as much as a very great number of facts which are badly observed and badly described".)

However, I am convinced that statistical data are useful and that in the long run reasoning is not scientifically and practically valid unless it leads to general propositions, although they must always be adapted to concrete situations.

It is not only the economy based on products and profits which has to be expressed statistically, however, but also the economy based on welfare. We have not yet succeeded in doing this.

For many years, the OECD has been progressing slowly towards the development of social indicators.

Recently, in the United States, one outstanding group[22] has suggested a means of calculating the "PQLI" (Physical Quality of Life Index). I myself prefer to speak of the "popular welfare index". What exactly is this?

The traditional measure of a country's economic progress—the Gross National Product (GNP) and its components—cannot provide any satisfactory estimate of the extent to which the needs of individuals are met.

The following observations give a clear indication of the need to design new measures of progress in the field of development:

1. The over-all GNP and the *per capita* GNP give no indication of the distribution of incomes.

2. The conceptual problems inherent in estimating income distribution in any society are even more complex in the case of developing countries, whose economies are largely rural and non-monetary.

3. Monetary measures in themselves give no indication of the levels of physical welfare of individuals, which is precisely the goal which planners of national and international development are trying to achieve.

During 1976 the Overseas Development Council studied various strategies of development and was particularly concerned with determining to what extent they are able to provide basic benefits to all classes of society. As a result of this study, a "physical quality of life index" was developed which would seem to be a useful tool for

[22] See Overseas Development Council, op. cit.

measuring the general progress achieved by a given country in satisfying, in a more equitable way, the fundamental human needs of the majority of the population.

The welfare index does not try to measure the many other social and psychological characteristics suggested by the expression "quality of life", such as justice, political liberty or the feeling of participation. It is based on the assumption that the needs and desires of individuals, at the initial stage and at the most fundamental level, are a longer life expectancy, more effective protection against sickness and better living conditions. This index measures not the volume of efforts made to achieve these objectives but rather the degree of their attainment, i.e. the results obtained. It takes into consideration the fact that there are various ways and means of progressing towards the satisfaction of these minimum needs—by improving nutrition, medical care and the distribution of income, by raising educational levels and by increasing employment.

Today, thanks to improvements made over long periods of time, the "developed" countries are generally able to guarantee to the greater part of their population reasonable levels of satisfaction of these basic requirements of human life. The countries of the Third World, for their part, must achieve a certain degree of satisfaction for each of these basic needs as quickly as possible. They will not succeed in doing this by copying the techniques and organizational methods of the industrialized countries but rather by choosing means which are suited to their own resources and their own culture. These means will necessarily vary widely, but they have one common objective: to provide better opportunities for social development to those who are most in need of them.

The studies of the Overseas Development Council are still in their initial stage and critical discussions are now being held about the methodology and basic criteria for calculating the welfare index. It is clear, however, that the three indicators of the ODC—life expectancy, infant mortality and literacy—can be used to measure the results of a wide range of policies. Values ranging from 1 to 100 are assigned to life expectancy, infant mortality and literacy, and the different countries are classified within this range according to their performance.

For the purposes of the study, the term "developing" describes all countries whose *per capita* income was less than $2000 in 1974 and/or whose welfare index was less than 90.[23]

In spite of the importance and high quality of these studies, however, it should perhaps be added that the three criteria in question have been chosen as significant by American experts who measure the value of life according to such indicators. They should no doubt be weighted in turn by other indicators chosen by non-Westerners in the light of values and reasons for living of different cultural universes.

If the economy finally succeeds in determining and satisfying these fundamental needs, if for this purpose we manage to calculate a popular welfare index for each environment, which not only comprises food, housing, clothing and health but also makes it possible to evaluate culture, security and freedom of thought, then we shall really have succeeded in rethinking the economy.[24]

This will call for many difficult research studies, but the need for them is imperative and urgent.

The violence of empires and the absence of supreme values

One of the greatest misfortunes of the Third World is that research there is considered a matter of secondary importance, that it is neglected and left to others who have the means and leisure to "waste" their time in laboratories.

For this reason, all the technologies in most of these countries are developed from abroad and this is of course where the term "transfer" of technology comes from.

Very few people seem to be alarmed by this trend, which in the long run leads to the disappearance of all will to autonomous development and independence. Instead of leaving professors, engineers and doctors to rot in prisons, instead of encouraging them to settle elsewhere, the farther away the better, they could be assigned to vast

---

[23] See a few useful tables in Appendix I which classify most countries according to income groups.

[24] In this connection reference may be made to J. Joblin, SJ: "Role of Human, Economic and Social Rights in the Advent of a New Society", in *Labour and Society* (Geneva, IILS), Vol. 2, No. 4, October 1977.

research programmes in viable regional centres. For those who do research also have a right to share in the fruits of development.

Empires of scientific and technical research are the most dangerous kind, as can be seen in the industrialized countries themselves. More and more monopolies are being created, which are controlled by the most powerful countries, and, eventually, by one alone. In this connection, the adventures and tribulations of the Concorde are highly significant. Whether the Anglo-French supersonic airplane can continue to land in New York is no longer the problem. But one thing is already clear: in view of the losses incurred and in spite of very great successes, it will be difficult for the countries concerned to maintain the techno-logical advance achieved, and their quasi-monopoly of research in this field, as in the nuclear field (whatever one may think of it), will be rivalled by strong developments elsewhere. [25]

When I talk about rethinking the economy, I want to encourage an awareness in the developing countries of the profound gravity of our situation in the World.

Paul-Marc Henry recently pointed out that less than 5 per cent of all scientific and technical research work is carried out in the countries of the Third World. However, it should be realized that research does not develop only in the laboratories of capital cities. Research is also the experience of a whole people, it includes the powers of observation of the peasants and the practical know-how of workers and craftsmen. And everybody is familiar with the ingenuity of the people in all kinds of fields. To mobilize these forces with a view to collective and co-ordinated research is a paramount, urgent and feasible task. Here again we can do a great deal with the little money at our disposal. Strict economy is a source of wealth.

However, in order to develop the type of.research which is within our reach, it behoves us to *reject* monopolies in this field by the big countries and big corporations, to reject this new kind of technological colonization which is already threatening Europe itself and with which the latter will threaten us much more seriously if it continues to restrict

---

[25] Concerning this, see *La France et ses mensonges* by F. de Closets (Paris, Denoël, 1977). See also the article by Jean Boissonnat in *Jeune Afrique*, No. 855 of 27 May 1977.

the access to world markets of our manufactured articles.[26] The empire of research and technology—that is clearly the greatest danger, and it takes its final form in the most highly perfected weapons for the most massive destruction. For one of the most scandalous paradoxes is to see poor and technically backward countries importing highly sophisticated weapons, and thus becoming completely dependent on the supplying countries on every plane—technical, economic and political.

If we permit the destruction of our peoples' ability to control their own environment, to feed themselves, to manufacture their tools and machinery, to build their houses, roads and means of transport, if we relegate them to a marginal role for the production of native handicrafts for tourists, we will really be destroying the chances of a living human community, we will be accepting the monologue of technology, which is the exact opposite of the dialogue of science and development.

In his "Discourse on Colonialism", Aimé Césaire has rightly drawn attention to a famous historian, Edgard Quinet, who wisely perceived the danger of the destruction of the original abilities of peoples, of their civilization and their creativity. It was Quinet, I think, who best described an empire in the final phase of the disintegration of cultures and techniques in the face of a technology which was abusively omnipresent although its universal sway was only temporary.[27]

---

[26] At its meeting held in Luxemburg in November 1977 the Club of Dakar, under the chairmanship of Mohamed Diawara, emphasized the abuses of growing protectionism in the industrialized countries and the unfortunate consequences of the resulting disturbances not only for the developing countries but also for the general balance of the world economy.

[27] "It is asked why barbarism emerged all of a sudden in ancient civilization. I think I can explain this. It is surprising that such a simple cause is not immediately apparent to everyone. The system of ancient civilization was composed of a certain number of nationalities and fatherlands, which, although they appeared to be enemies or even did not know each other, nevertheless protected, supported and watched out for each other. When the Roman empire grew larger and set about conquering and destroying these bodies of nations, the amazed sophists thought they saw, at the end of this road, humanity triumphant in Rome. There was talk about the unity of the human mind: that was only a dream. It turned out that these nationalities were only so many ramparts which were protecting Rome itself. When, therefore, in this alleged triumphal march towards one civilization, Rome had destroyed, one after the other, Carthage,

The violent convulsions which are occurring in a world which the economy has made prosperous for some and a living hell for others suggest that we must look for different solutions.

According to Malraux, "the absence of supreme values" is the cause of the dangers in which we are already engulfed. One of these supreme values is undoubtedly the spirit of research, the development of the intellect. For once man has been freed from the bondage of money, it is only just that he be restored to real life and all its possibilities through the exercise of his intelligence.

It is for this reason I have suggested that we ought to rethink the economy. But that will not be enough. What is also needed is the *will*, the will to "change", and to prove to ourselves the power of poverty.

Egypt, Greece, Judea, Persia, Dacia and the Gauls, it turned out that it had itself eaten away the walls which were protecting it against the human flood beneath which it was to perish. By crushing the Gauls, mighty Caesar only opened the way to the Germans. The annihilation of all those societies, the extinction of all those languages, cities, laws and homes created a vacuum around Rome, and in those places which were not reached by the barbarians, barbarism came about by itself. When the Gauls were destroyed, they became the Bagaudae. Thus the violent fall and gradual eradication of particular cities brought about the collapse of ancient civilization. That social edifice had been supported by nationalities like so many different marble or porphyry columns. "When each of those living columns had been destroyed, amid the applause of the wise men of the time, the edifice fell to the ground and the wise men of our own time are still trying to find out how it was possible for such great ruins to have been made at one moment!"

CHAPTER IV

Lords of the Morning Dew
or
Poverty in Power

"The land is a battle day after day, a battle without respite: clearing the land, sowing, weeding and watering, until the harvest, and then one morning you see your ripe field lying before you all covered with dew, and you say: that's what I am, lord of the morning dew . . . "

(Jacques Roumain)

"Sabedlo, soberanos y vasallos, próceres y mendigos: nadie tendrá derecho a lo superfluo mientras alguien carezca de lo estricto."

(Salvador Díaz Mirón: "Asonancias", in his collection, *Poesías: Primera Epoca*)

[Know, O ye sovereigns and vassals, Noblemen and beggars, No-one shall have a right to the superfluous As long as anyone wants for the bare necessities.]

I began this book by quoting from the Bible and the Koran among other sources. I shall perhaps be blamed for it. But I am only following the logic of my chosen line of argument. The concept of poverty acquires a special resonance in the context of religion which still remains a reality for the majority of people—both believers and unbelievers. I therefore return now to those sources to throw light upon a significant contemporary phenomenon.

Figures in the public eye, held up by the mass media for our daily contemplation and . . . admiration, are well aware of the danger of letting any inconsistency appear in their image.

90

While change is a sign of life, and a change may be for the better, it becomes a serious matter if it takes the form of a betrayal of the self. In my view this is what has happened to *Marcel Lefebvre.*

In search of lost power . . .

The former missionary who is such a controversial figure today is probably unaware that I listened to him with great interest in a college in Ouidah which he used to visit. Later, as a student in Dakar, I lived in his "diocese" for 4 years. I was very moved at the time by the way he preached faithfulness and absolute obedience to the "successor of Peter *whoever he may be*", he himself being the Pope's official representative for "French Africa and Madagascar".

Yet already beneath his great piety there were glimpses of a kind of sickness, a disease to which he has now succumbed to the point where it may even affect his faculties of self-criticism. The bishop who denounced "the only unforgivable sin—the sin against the spirit" seems to have forgotten some of his religious vows. . . .

In fact, more than his vows, what seems to concern him most is the POWER which he once exercised in the name of the True Faith as archbishop, apostolic delegate for a whole continent, superior general of a religious order in Rome, and so forth. He appears, indeed, to have been so strongly motivated by this power—which was temporal quite as much as spiritual, evidenced by scarlet rochets, jewelled mitres and glittering crosiers—that when he was deprived of it by circumstances, or perhaps also by that refusal to admit contradiction which some people feel has always characterized him in spite of appearances to the contrary, he had to find a new field of action— still in the name of the True Faith—for expressing those certainties which make dogma, belief and above all habit so immensely reassuring. No matter if this involves fraternizing with the *Action française* and its present-day successors. No matter if the vows of poverty and obedience are broken. . . . The money coming in, the regained authority, the publicity which distracts but makes one a celebrity— all this apparently outweighs the problem of the trusting followers who naively believe that the whole question lies in the "mass in Latin", a language which in any case hardly anyone any longer speaks

or understands. If this were not the case, Virgil and his famous inter-
jection would no doubt have been invoked in the language of the
clerics long ago. But now that the *Aeneid* and its gods are completely
forgotten, we must settle for having the stanzas of the *Lutrin* dinned
into our ears—celebrating "battles and the dread priest" whose
extravagance and anathemas would be amusing if they did not in fact
raise in all seriousness the disquieting question: "How can so much
venom exist in the souls of the faithful?"[1]

The dangers of counter-development

What has happened to Marcel Lefebvre can be seen every day in
societies where the passion for power has become an obsession which
impairs judgement and particularly where true values are replaced by
false ones and the result is an artificial life cut off from local surroundings. It is a situation from which a large number of Third
World countries are suffering today.

There is no longer any need to establish the evidence that the policies
followed so far have been a failure, and that little progress has been
made in combating death, disease, ignorance and social fragmentation.
The facts in these respects give little cause for satisfaction. We can
now state clearly that the kind of power which determines our policies
and informs our action programmes is very often incompatible with
the priorities and objectives at which we ought to be aiming. What is
more, as we have already seen, it is a power which sometimes illustrates
another reality, that of counter-development.

I have dwelt at some length in earlier pages on the current cult of
the trappings of power, the palaces, the motor-cycle escorts, the
titles, medals and fireworks, and above all the ubiquitous worship
of money. In a recent television broadcast a Swiss journalist asked
a peasant from Gruyère what he felt constituted the glory of a nation,
an institution or a human life. "Glory?" said the peasant throwing up
his hands, "What an empty word!"

The remark deserves attention, especially if we are seeking practical
ways and means, as well as a valid theory, that will set us free and

[1] Cf. Virgil: *Aeneid*, I, 11, and Boileau: *Le lutrin*, I, 1-12.

enable us to build a society with the necessary cohesive force to meet the basic needs of all its members. It is imperative to examine the nature of power to ensure that it corresponds with our chosen objectives.

Clearly the changes required will depend on a new political will.

The high purpose of what I am trying to say can best be illustrated by an analogy. We have inherited a particular type of power; it was colonial power founded on the will to conquer of the nations; it leads to convictions like the belief that military might is the offspring of affluence and the ultimate proof of superiority. In one of the books which has had the most influence on my own education, *The Arrogance of Power*, former American senator William Fulbright stresses the harm which such concepts have done to the world. He recalls, for example, how the United States went to war with Spain in 1898 with the apparent aim of liberating Cuba from the Spanish yoke but with the final consequence not only of placing the island under their own protection but of annexing the Philippines as well, since "according to President McKinley, the Lord told him it was America's duty 'to educate the Filipinos, and uplift and civilize and Christianize them'. . ."[2]

The Americans of the time were thus a conquering race and would certainly have agreed with Albert Beveridge when he said: "We must obey our blood and occupy new markets and if necessary new lands" because "in the Almighty's infinite plan . . . debased civilizations and decaying races" must disappear "before the higher civilization of the nobler and more virile types of man".[3]

After drawing attention to these historical facts, Fulbright points out that the consequences are still to be felt today for Americans, especially when they are abroad, feel that they belong to the richest nation in the world and can therefore behave worse than they would at home. Here Fulbright touches on something which he seems to feel very deeply: "One reason Americans abroad may act as though they 'own the place' is that in many places they very nearly do: American companies may dominate large segments of a country's economy; American products are advertised on billboards and displayed in shop windows; American hotels and snack bars are available to protect

[2] J. William Fulbright: *The Arrogance of Power* (New York, Random House, 1966), p. 6.

[3] Ibid., pp. 6-7.

American tourists from foreign influence; American soldiers may be stationed in the country, and even if they are not, the population are probably well aware that their very survival depends on the wisdom with which America uses her immense military power.''[4]

Riches through money; social well-being confined to the rich; protection of the rich by the power of arms: such is the three-fold basis of colonial or imperial power.

Clearly, as Fulbright suggests, this leads to the "fatal impact" which the rich and powerful inflict on the rest of the world. "Dependent on it though the Vietnamese are, American strength is a reproach to their weakness, American wealth a mockery of their poverty."[5]

And so we see the Vietnamese reduced to letting their wives and daughters work as barmaids, ready to do anything for the foreign soldiers who have so much money to throw about; taxi-drivers preferring to pick up Americans who will pay any fare, however outrageous; and in a remarkably short time barmaids, prostitutes, pimps and taxi-drivers find themselves at the top of the economic pyramid. As a result, houses and apartments are no longer to be had because rents have become "Americanized"; ordinary people of all kinds are unable to make ends meet owing to the galloping inflation. The time is ripe for a social upheaval. As a Vietnamese told a representative of the *New York Times*: "Any time legions of prosperous white men descend on a rudimentary Asian society, you are bound to have trouble".[6]

Indeed, all that is simple and traditional collapses under the impact of wealth and power. It is indeed a fatal impact since the vast majority of people desire dignity and independence, "not the honour of a supine role in an American empire".

The duty of freedom

I mentioned an analogy. Let us return to it. Just as it was necessary to achieve freedom from the will to power of the nations in the form of colonial imperialism with its attendant confiscation of property, excessive accumulation of other people's wealth, and private owner-

[4] J. William Fulbright, op. cit., p. 10.

[5] J. William Fulbright, op. cit., p. 16.

[6] J. William Fulbright, op. cit., pp. 16-17.

ship of collective resources; just as it is necessary, as Fulbright points
out, to escape from the "welfare imperialism" and reject the passionate
pursuit of extravagant goals which ends by reducing people to slavery
and denying them the very right to exist; so in each country, and
particularly the least favoured ones, the need arises for a struggle
against the formation of a dominant group of individuals who,
whether deliberately or not, gain control of the national heritage—
a fight against the consolidation of institutions and structures which
allow an élite to govern in selfish ease while others merely have the
privilege of some subordinate role. All this must be done away with.
Yet nothing will be achieved without a revolution at the level of the
individual, the emergence of a new political will based on what I have
called the duty of freedom.[7] This deliberate and sought-after revolution
is precisely: *Poverty in Power*.

It may be necessary to give some further explanation.

In 1964 when I was engaged in research on political science at the
Harvard Centre for International Affairs, Henry Kissinger suggested
that we should read the outstanding work by Karen Horney: *The
Neurotic Personality of our Time*. In this book which dates from
1937 the author describes the three perils involved in the competitive
struggle of modern man to maintain the social status imposed by the
psychosis of accumulation: "—aggressiveness grown so pronounced
that it cannot be reconciled with Christian brotherhood; —desire for
material goods so vigorously stimulated that it cannot be satisfied;
—expectations of untrammeled freedom soaring so high that they
cannot be squared with the multitudes of responsibilities and restrictions
that confine us all".

And the corollary of these perils is the violence which erupts in
a society which has become no better than a jungle, and the need to
strengthen the police and all other so-called security services.

One thing emerges clearly from an examination of the statistics
quoted in the last chapter: that in all regions of the world, expenditure
on education is distinctly lower than expenditure on armaments.

[7] Here I should like to draw attention to a remark by Françoise Giroud in *La comédie
du pouvoir* (Paris, Fayard, 1977): ". . . to give up freedom of thought, the most
important possession of all, is to give up altogether". And so to abandon our human
status. Here we are far from comedy. What a tragedy, indeed!

Exceptions in a few regions merely confirm the general rule that power depends on force and violence.

It would be naive to think that it is possible to do without a responsible national defence. Certainly in some cases people have no other choice but recourse to arms, a fact which is confirmed every day in the whole of southern Africa. But obviously, this is not the real problem. What is dangerous is the exponential growth of destructive weapons, very often in countries which may never be attacked at all. In many areas the frantic production of arms is intended for the sole purpose of exerting control over the citizens and keeping them in training.

Luckily other examples exist.

Thus, Costa Rica has no army. I shall be reminded that the country suffers from other problems. It is nevertheless true that it is possible, at least in theory, and taking Costa Rica as an example, to imagine countries with no army, countries whose principal resources are devoted in the first place to the positive goal of meeting basic needs.

In fact the force of arms merely serves to back up the insatiable desire for accumulation of material possessions. This often leads to the corruption of those in power since their only aim is the pursuit of money by every possible means, including embezzlement of funds or resources; underhand arrangements with suppliers, heads of firms and company directors; and secret rakeoffs and compensatory returns for supplying information to foreign secret services. It would be only too easy to elaborate this point and to list names, dates and places. . . . But that is not our purpose. I am only touching on the subject in order to confirm the conviction that it is not possible to build a society on the corruption of political leaders, the prostitution of schoolgirls, the theft of goods belonging to the State and the general violation of law and conscience. I am not painting too black a picture by leaving out the glimmers of hope. I am describing well-known situations which are typical of power in a large number of societies where the leaders, in order to preserve the liberties they have usurped, abuse the authority entrusted to them and set up dictatorships and fascist systems. Then comes the long and hideous train of imprisonment, torture, murder and sometimes even wholesale slaughter. There is no need to go into further detail: all this is common knowledge. The International Law Commission regularly publishes information, issues warnings and sometimes even manages to capture our attention.[8]

In order to remain unchallenged, this *nouveau riche* style of power must suppress information and stifle criticism. Governments therefore decide what the "children" who are their subjects may read, censoring books, newspapers and study programmes. We have returned to the days of the deliberate fostering of ignorance.[9]

Once again, there are echoes of Georges Hardy: "Education in the colonies can never be too limited. The danger is not of teaching too little but of teaching too much. . . ." Education is not, however, confined to the school, it is also a matter of enlightened public opinion. We must admit that direct or indirect denunciations, which the International Commission of Human Rights has not always been able to keep secret, have revealed that we have sometimes shown the most despicable mediocrity and stupidity in manipulating facts, ideas and beliefs— in the name, of course, of pretentious "revolutionary" slogans. . . .

Clearly these slogans are not enough to produce the promised or desired results. Alexis de Tocqueville once denounced the semblance of power which, like "the external appearance of strength, may sometimes sustain a feeble body, but usually ends by crushing it".

If it is not possible for philosophers to assume power, then at least political leaders should learn philosophy. This, of course, was Plato's opinion, convinced as he was of the excellence of philosophy for the conduct of human affairs.

A State attuned to the voice of the people

In any society the State is responsible for administering power while directly or indirectly also exercising it. But the State is not a natural

---

[8] In a recent book, *La philosophie africaine* (Paris, Maspero, 1977), Paulin Hountondji writes: "When the vice of terror is everywhere tightened, the kind of terror which takes away the breath and dries the mouth; when all speech becomes dangerous, risking the worst kind of brutality and sometimes even loss of life; when the insolent machinery of the neo-colonial states is everywhere triumphant, with its train of intimidation, arbitrary arrest, torture, legal assassination, stifling all true thought at the source, the official ideologist belches contentedly: our ancestors would have shouted alleluia!" (p. 239).

[9] "To such an extent", writes the same author, "that there is a very real danger that we will soon be forbidden, in the name of Marxism, to read the works of Marx" (p. 257).

being or independent entity. It ought to be the organized embodiment of the converging will of the citizens, set up for the express purpose of furthering their aims.

I should like to explain what I mean by taking the somewhat unexpected example of the termites' nest.

A termites' nest is like a body—a single body of which the termites are merely the limbs. This means that termites have no freedom: no termite is capable of taking any initiative which is not in keeping with the conduct of the nest as a whole or the activity of a given group of termites—the soldiers for example—since the group itself merely represents one aspect of the overall purpose of the whole. Consequently the queen as "Head of State" or as the focal point of the total energy in the nest is endowed with all the necessary means for accomplishing her "duty" and achieving the relevant goals. Research has shown that the entire social life of the termites' nest is controlled by the queen who uses telepathy to convey information to the different parts of the nest which function like the limbs of a body of which she is the brain. If the queen is killed the termites immediately cease to know where to go or what to do: so they in their turn can only die.

The example of the termites' nest is not only surprising but could be used to support theories of management and models of society diametrically opposed to the ones I am in fact advocating. I should like to reassure the reader and merely use the analogy to illustrate an elementary but essential lesson in biology, that power must always be *of the same nature as those on whose behalf it is exercised.*

If we could solve the problem of the nature of power and those who share in it at no matter what level, this would ensure harmony among the different groups which make up our society. It becomes easier to understand why Alain reached the conclusion that "left to itself, all power goes mad". All power for power's sake ends by destroying itself. There can be no lasting power among men which is not freely acknowledged and used in the service of mankind.

In a country where the majority of people suffer from unemployment, hunger, disease and illiteracy, power, unless it is completely self-centred, can only be the reflection of the general situation. Identification with the needs of the whole community confers legitimacy upon it and provides the basis for the necessary structural changes. If, on the other hand, power is the preserve of the rich and privileged, it is bound to incur the "fatal impact" for, as *The Little Prince*[10] warns us, authority is based on reason, and: "if you order your people to throw themselves into the sea, you are bound to have a revolution on your hands".

The concept of "poverty in power" as I have just described it involves several different stages of reflection and action. It may be useful, for example, to consider the following three topics:

—Simplicity of the State and its machinery in order to ensure improved popular participation in the decision-making process;

—Social organization based on decentralization, and independent and sometimes collective management of essential resources;

—Role of the school system and popular know-how.

A policy of self-reliant community development based on satisfaction of the basic needs of the population clearly implies the participation of that population, men, women and children, at all levels, beginning at the place in which they live.

Participation presupposes a certain number of conditions—a political will on the part of the leaders, the élite and the population as a whole; genuine national unity; the possibility of two-way communication between rulers and ruled, as well as laterally, between members of the same group; permanent structures of organization, assessment and control; and a broad system of general education and information.

Not only are these prerequisites inextricably interwoven, they are all equally indispensable.

Human progress is determined not by material conditions alone, but also by ideas. "Right ideas", said Mao Tse-tung, "can become, once they penetrate the masses, an immense material force capable of transforming the world." A policy of poverty practised and preached by honest rulers and officials could become a tremendous regenerating force in society.

This kind of political will stems from a simple statement: "I want to be master of my own destiny", and requires an answer to a more complex question: "In order to do so, what do I need most?—a well-

---

[10] A. de Saint-Exupéry.

drilled army, a fleet of 'Mirages'? my own efforts or those of other people working in co-operation with me?''

If the political leaders live simply, without shutting themselves up in sumptuous palaces and surrounding themselves by a court of pompous officials, their example will be of inestimable value to the ordinary people who will soon realize that they are not the only ones to make sacrifices, but that poverty is genuinely experienced and shared by all.

In this context the little State of Papua-New Guinea recently set an example of integrity by refusing to allow four embassies to be set up on its territory because of the excessive expenditure which this would have entailed for the country. The government of Papua-New Guinea, lacking the resources to "welcome" new diplomatic missions, refused permission to the USSR, China, France and the Republic of Korea to open embassies in the capital, Port Moresby, since the size of the Department of Foreign Affairs would have had to be doubled to meet the corresponding increase in staff and expenditure.

Unless the rulers have the courage to set an example by sharing poverty, the people will not take declarations of equality and fraternity seriously. Indeed, the public is never slow to recognize the sincerity of speeches and intentions. A foreigner who speaks the local language can often learn more about the mood of a town or village from a rapid walk through the market than from any number of conversations in the offices of the capital.

Once the wives of ministers and high officials in any country stop going to the market themselves, they cut themselves off from what I am convinced is one of the most important lines of communication in our societies. The result is, of course, that they are losing an opportunity for assisting their husbands in the exercise of their functions.

Joseph Fontanet, a man with considerable political experience, in a recent work, *Le social et le vivant*, emphasizes the importance of this basic system of communication:

> "The Greek city is incomprehensible without the existence of the agora; Rome is incomprehensible if one deliberately ignores the role of the forum. For the agora, the forum and the market are essentially meeting places, in other words opportunities for

the exchange of information. . . . In the market place goods are traded, prices are fixed and information and rumours exchanged concerning the movements of the king, the appointment of officials and the relative strength of different factions. And, directly, this whole process which might be described as "rumour" has an impact on prices, affects the briskness or otherwise of trade, and in fact creates the background against which decisions will subsequently be taken. Rumour influences decisions and sometimes anticipates them; decisions in turn feed rumour.''

This is equally true of our own societies where the tom-tom is heard in the market place whence it is rapidly transmitted in the form of bush telegraph.[11] Moreover it is essential that the authorities should listen to rumours, not in order to forestall revolts but to be able to formulate their policy in accordance with popular wishes.

Leaders in constant communication with their people would be like planners responsible for achieving within a given time certain specific social targets, discussed by everyone and decided on by the majority. The political leaders would above all be leaders of the social life of the country.

Planning open to all

At national level, a policy aimed at self-reliant development would take the form of a plan for integrated growth based on the genuine needs to be met.

We have already called attention to the fact that this kind of planning requires drawing up a systematic inventory of resources and fixing targets which are of a primarily social nature.

If we think of the plan not as a kind of "open sesame" but as an instrument of prospective policy—the art of government, after all, lies in foreseeing the future, not just living from day to day—we should then be able to avoid hazardous enterprises, rough guesswork and wastage. Every developing country knows by now that it must have:

[11] The kind of rumour which anticipates official information. The rumour may give rise to interesting discussions . . . equally, it may encourage idle gossip which only distracts attention from genuine problems.

—an investment and employment plan based on sectoral or regional programmes;

—a national development plan for the organization of the national territory for both physical and social infrastructure programmes;

—a plan for adapting government and administrative structures to the material and human requirements of the society concerned.

But planning must be flexible: it should constitute an essential frame of reference without stifling initiative and responsibility at the source.

Only a contract of solidarity between members of the community as a whole can ensure intelligent planning for the satisfaction of the genuine needs of each individual, while rejecting privilege and inequality.

If this kind of planning is to be effective, it must come out from behind the closed doors of the ministries where it remains the prerogative of the few. Public participation is indispensable: organized at local and regional level it should encompass all other forms of participation—in production, health, education and study of local conditions. Strongly influenced by the people's views, it must inevitably be approved by them. At local level it involves confronting specific community needs and aspirations with the overall targets defined at national level.

It is also important to set up bodies responsible for long-term thinking, not cumbersome and costly organizations of bureaucrats, but institutions which enable young and old, men and women to think for themselves, express their views and begin to plan for the future.

The general discussion which took place in Algeria before the adoption of the draft National Charter would seem to provide a successful example of the attempt to stimulate communication between the people at large and the planners and executives, whatever their position in the community.

The means for achieving growth are of course technical—we speak of planning natural resources or planned production—but human beings alone are the driving force behind development, as they are its main purpose and ultimate *raison d'être*: human beings alone can make riches bear fruit. It is men who invent, create, organize, build. We must therefore give priority to planning human resources. The process begins with a demographic study which enables us to evaluate quantitatively and qualitatively the primary object of development: man as producer and consumer, the social being who seeks to organize a harmonious and close-knit community.

A great many developing countries have recognized the importance of demography, and drawn up programmes and plans in which population statistics are incorporated as vital factors in the theory and action required for economic and social development.

Knowledge and command of demographic principles are essential in countries undergoing a population explosion.

At the same time, any policy of birth control must remain secondary to the main priority which is the deliberate building of a society based on the goals which are desired or accepted by everyone. These include in the first place satisfaction of immediate needs by working to produce more collective wealth and ensuring that it is shared out with increasing fairness. If China, by a regime of strict economy, has succeeded in raising its standard of living, it is mainly because no one dies of hunger any more. It is precisely because it has been possible to co-ordinate the efforts of the people to combat extreme poverty that the population growth has slowed down. Only when people are concerned for the education of their children and feel responsible for their future does contraception become a reality. No form of direct action can be effective on its own unless conditions and prospects exist for improved material and cultural well-being. [12]

Politics is not merely a technique to gain or keep power or run the economy from above: it is above all a people's ability to organize themselves so as to have the means of choosing, criticizing and reflecting on the aims to be pursued; it is making each individual personally responsible for the running of all social activities through various forms of delegation and representation.

In Europe private ownership of land only developed in the eighteenth century when the English nobles decided to enclose their property.

---

[12] See G. Blardone: *"Note de prospective sociale*: Quelques réflexions concernant la relation croissance démographique—développement"*, Institut de Sciences sociales appliquées, Lyon, 17 May 1977.

Other extremely interesting remarks on the subject will be found in *People: an international choice* by Rafael M. Salas, Executive Director of the United Nations Fund for Population Activities (Oxford, Pergamon Press, 1977).

"Private property was born", says Jean-Jacques Rousseau, "on the day when a man who had enclosed a field decided to say:—'this is mine'—and found people stupid enough to believe him." The physiocrats were among the first to proclaim the doctrine of maximum profitability of landed property, a doctrine which led to increasing poverty in the countryside and so released the work-force necessary for the burgeoning industrial revolution. Only by exploiting the poor and destitute was such a "revolution" made possible.

The fortune of the industrialized countries was founded in the first place on poverty at home, before it expanded by means of the exploitation of the rest of the world.

The fortune of the élite of the Third World is based on the same process. Private ownership of resources tends to perpetuate inequality.

On the other hand, with a democratic concept based on poverty for the individual and maximum wealth for the community, a different kind of organization would make it possible to reduce needs and satisfy them without inciting the kind of violence which injustice always arouses.

Decentralization and participation

If we want to persuade the people to participate in a particular scheme, the best method is certainly not to harass them and upset their habits on the pretext of obtaining rapid visible results. It is better to wait until everyone feels personally involved in a programme established both with the consent of the group and by the group.

The first stage of studying local conditions ensures evaluation and expression of needs; selection and training of leaders from the group is one prerequisite for self-management. But there are others:

—acquisition by all of the knowledge and authority required for the efficient operation of production;

—dissemination of information by local leaders, political parties, the press and radio;

—assurance of economic control once the cost, acquisition and operation of the means of production are within reach of those concerned.

If the local population is to assume effective responsibility, it must be in charge of running the operation, with authority to make adjustments in the light of the results obtained.

Clearly, therefore, a policy of decentralization is indispensable in the context of self-reliant development where everyone must be responsible at his own particular level for the well-being of the groups to which he or she belongs—work groups, or specific groups of women, young people, village community, and so on. Centralized States, as we know, tend to generate cumbersome bureaucracies which stifle all initiative at local level. A decentralized structure, on the other hand, brings the decision-making centres closer to the people and releases creative energy.

Decentralization is aimed in the first place at giving local communities, the inhabitants of a village for example, full responsibility for dealing with all problems of local interest. Secondly, as the basic units of planning, these communities take part in the formulation and implementation of development strategy and regional planning. Thus in Algeria "Operation 1000 villages" has been mounted with a view both to rebuilding the old villages, the "douars", destroyed during the war, and setting up independent communities with adequate facilities for everyone to live, work and receive education and training on the spot. An attempt is made to preserve the architectural style of the villages while at the same time making more space available for community life such as public squares or cultural centres.

Decentralization is not merely a device for shifting problems to another level. The danger is that the central power will delegate part of its authority to the local assemblies without giving them the funds to exercise it. Unless the local and regional communities have the financial resources to carry out their own policies, no amount of authority and freedom to take decisions will be of any use.

A two-fold difficulty remains: attempts to decentralize power constantly run the risk of being used to divide the people. At the same time, although they are in themselves essential, efforts to re-organize the underprivileged are always in danger of leading merely to another form of concentration of power which is once more seized by a handful of individuals. When this happens power becomes totally resistant to further change.

In order to remedy the situation, people everywhere have introduced formal rules, laws, systems of checks and balances, public assemblies. But these safeguards are not enough: they can so easily become ineffective unless each and every individual is imbued with a sense of responsibility towards the community. Rules can be bent without difficulty once rulers and people alike lose sight of the social role attributed to each individual and the need to re-examine the distribution of these roles and constantly re-allocate functions in the light of the agreed aims of participation.

Checks and balances, discussions in organizations, political parties, citizens' committees and public assemblies all have an essential part to play. Yet I must emphasize their utopian nature: even with the best citizens' committees, the clearest lines of communication between public and politicians, even if the strictest sanctions are in force against corruption—nothing can provide a substitute for the other condition of the contract: *the honesty of those in power.* External control is not enough, there must also be integrity within. Political and social leaders are vital factors in the transformation of society. If the raw material is rotten, the end product cannot be good.

If power is to operate satisfactorily, the partners in the social contract must be able to review the situation at regular intervals to avoid undue complacency with the *status quo.* All effective religious and philosophical systems make provision for discussion and re-assessment in various different ways: self-criticism, evaluation, etc. China, for example, has its cultural revolution. . . .

Re-assessment releases liberating energy. It is important to make it a regular procedure. A well-balanced society can never be taken for granted, it must be fought for every day.

If no provision is made for discussion or checks and balances, any government will sooner or later be tempted to abuse its power. But liberalization of public life and institutions will only be possible provided that education goes hand in hand with economic development. In order to rescue a people from destitution it is not enough to satisfy material needs. Cultural deprivation alone can jeopardize the practice of democracy.

Education for all: foundation of democracy,
fulcrum of development

No political awareness, no adherence to a blueprint for society, no communication can exist if a population is kept in ignorance. The power of the poor lies above all in their knowledge. Illiteracy often provides a pretext for coercion. There is no doubt that if no effort is made to educate the people, participation is difficult to achieve.

The right to education and training is as much a basic need as a decent standard of living.

If we agree with Schultz and Galbraith that nowhere in the world is there an illiterate peasantry which is favourable to progress, nor an educated peasantry which is unfavourable to progress, education will be seen to be highly productive—provided that it is allowed to fulfil its true role of increasing the all-round ability and enhancing the value of human beings.

As early as 1924, a survey carried out by "Gosplan" in the USSR showed that one year of apprenticeship in a factory increased the production of an illiterate worker by only 12 to 16 per cent, whereas one year of primary school increased it by 30 per cent and four years of primary school increased it by 79 per cent.

In 1924 the education budget was 1622 million roubles. Ten years later a study showed that the growth in national income due to the increased productivity of workers who had received only primary education was as much as 2000 million roubles. Thus the priority given to general education in the USSR, by indirectly ensuring a higher level of occupational skill, in fact acted as the main catalyst for development.

In the Third World, governments are everywhere making laudable efforts to promote education and literacy among both children and adults. One of the main problems they come up against is devising an efficient training system for self-reliant community development. In this context the re-organization of elementary education should be aimed at ensuring that the school becomes a centre of rural development, by giving the teacher—who should also contribute towards adult education—a leading role in the community.

One or two interesting experiments have already been carried out.

In Senegal, the 2 years' intermediate education is aimed at giving children in rural areas practical training in agricultural problems to make it easier for them to settle into their own village and work there. Girls are taught hygiene, nutrition and child care, and of course general education, which remains essential.

Similar experiments have been carried out in Tanzania.

Mr. Julius Nyerere writes: "We realised that we had to build up a doctrine so as to be able to carry on, and we changed completely the teaching methods in primary schools. Now, we help the children first to understand their problems; then they realise on their own that new methods are needed to solve them."[13]

Educational reform should be undertaken on the basis of the kind of faculties which must be developed in the individuals to enable them to make an impact on their physical or economic environment.

Professional people of all kinds are needed for self-reliant and self-managed development. Teachers, agronomists, technicians of various kinds, doctors and nutritionists must help the peasants to help themselves in the fight against endemic disease and malnutrition.

In order to avoid a rift between the professional classes and the rest of the population, we shall have to impose, as is already done in some countries, an interchange of activities and a combination of manual and intellectual work.

In Cuba, for example, medical students must do other jobs connected with medicine throughout the whole period of their studies. During the first 2 years when they are acquiring basic knowledge, they act as part-time orderlies. In the course of the next 2 years they are used as nurses, and it is only at the end of the 2 final years that they are allowed to assist the doctors. On completion of the 6 years' training, they must first practise in a rural area. At the end of each 2-year period, they are free to break off their studies and are given a diploma corresponding to the level they have reached and the activity they are qualified to perform.

The major task of education, in fact, is teaching people how to learn, how to become fitted to cope with change.

In 1978 a child is being educated for a working life which may

---

[13] Quoted in René Dumont and Marcel Mazoyer: *Développement et socialismes* (Paris, Editions du Seuil, 1969).

last until 2030 or later. It is thus more than likely that the average citizen will have to assimilate a large number of new techniques in the course of his life.

Specialization, the search for efficiency without sacrificing general culture, the development of mental aptitudes to promote a better understanding of tasks which lie ahead; these are the basic principles which ought to replace the current methods of education which do little to help men and women to escape from their destitute condition.

The problem of destitution will only be solved if there exist professional classes who are close to the people, aware of the part they must play and ready to make the necessary sacrifices. Unless the professional people are familiar with the living conditions of the very poor, unless they establish close contact with them, the art of the possible will be lost and all that will remain will be an "ivory tower" kind of social revolution or planning policy.

An Indian sociologist, Mr. Srinivas, notes that with a few honourable exceptions, the economists in his country study rural life on the basis of various reports, censuses and sample surveys but "they never think of going into the field themselves. . . . This attitude seems strange, since they are very anxious to put an end to the exploitation of the poor . . . and yet these praiseworthy aims do not seem to incite them to enter into close contact with those whom they wish to help."[14]

Yet you probably learn more through self-education and practical experience than in any other way. It is only by discussions at all levels and practical application of the results that a people aware of its own strength will gradually be able to develop.

Thus in order to achieve a permanent mobilization of public opinion, education and guidance are needed through the structures set up to encourage development at community level.

Participation and local leadership: "ladies first . . ."

Self-reliant community development means releasing the potential energy of the people at all levels and harnessing it in support of the activities of the public authorities.

---

[14] Gilbert Etienne: "Le débat sur la pauvreté rurale dans le tiers monde", in *Annales d'études internationales*, No. 7, Geneva, 1976.

In recent years a great deal of interest has been shown in problems of rural social participation in Africa, Latin America and Asia. The basic principles have, moreover, evolved and certain authoritarian forms of intervention in peasant life are now condemned, while greater emphasis is laid on knowledge of local conditions in any particular community.

At present it is generally recognized that any policy for self-reliant development must take account of the following four factors:
—knowledge of local conditions;
—local leadership;
—organization of the population;
—training local leaders.

Every method used must be the result of on-going research. There is no ready-made formula. The policy adopted in each country, each region, each village will require constant adjustment depending on the reactions of the different groups and the specific local conditions.

Experience gained in the course of a programme of women's education for rural development in the Republic of Niger from 1966 to 1975 will provide a basis for discussion of possible methods and an indication of the kind of problems which may arise. [15]

Women's participation in development is, like that of their menfolk or young people, a key factor in the struggle to escape from the type of development whose aim is the accumulation of wealth, in order to create a society based on shared poverty.

States which encourage women to take part in development are ensuring their own survival and contributing towards the establishment of a free and flourishing society.

On the other hand, progress is impossible if women are left out of development projects, if their needs are ignored and they are excluded from any kind of political discussion.

In order to get to know the women and share their reflections on their living conditions and day-to-day problems, the women officers

---

[15] *La participation des femmes rurales au développement*, IRAM, 49 rue de la Glacière, Paris XIIIe. For all the questions I raise here concerning participation, education for development or decentralization, reference can now be made to a very useful book—Albert Meister: *La participation pour le développement* (Paris, Editions Economie et Humanisme, Les Editions Ouvrières, 1978).

of the Niger rural social participation service went to live in the villages and took part in local life.

The initial contact always required prior permission from the men, whether or not they were already aware of the need for their wives to play a part in local development. Their attitude was that "the women's place is behind the man, but not too far behind".

After the overall survey which served to initiate the programme, specific studies were carried out on childbirth, agriculture, livestock raising, groundnut oil processing, malaria, etc. The women were interviewed as they gathered around the well, beneath the tree where they threshed the millet, or in the course of local meetings, and when the results were later placed before the community as a whole, they proved useful as a basis for analysing the various causes of the problems and deciding on the action to be taken at two different levels: by the village on its own or with assistance from outside.

In this kind of operation, leadership can be organized in one of two ways: either by using village-level officials like extension officers, or by choosing leaders from among the peasants themselves.

The second system is preferable for a policy of self-reliance. In Latin America, and Colombia in particular, an attempt is made to find the natural leaders in a group and encourage them to provide the initiative for self-reliant development. Specialized officials do have a part to play but at a different level: by training local leaders, providing support for their activities and drawing up programmes for areas covering several villages.

In some African countries officials are called in to organize the choice of local leaders. Women leaders are chosen as a function of:

—traditional status: e.g. the wife of the headman, traditionally responsible for women in the village;

—social and economic status;

—technical ability: skill in a specific field.

The local midwife is often chosen for the numerous services she is able to render.

The qualifications needed for a midwife to be selected for training are as follows:

—practical experience;

—she must not be too old to learn new techniques;

—discretion;
—authority and influence;
—permanent residence in the village;
—the husband's consent.

Training for women village leaders takes the form of short courses. General and specific instruction is provided on problems affecting the village (for example, women from rural areas are taught about weaning, home hygiene, malaria, etc.).

Clearly this is the beginning of an interesting experiment but there is a danger that, if care is not taken, it may lead to knowledge and power becoming concentrated in the hands of the "richest" people under the present system.

The wife of the former Mauritanian head of state, Mrs. Moktar Ould Daddah, who has made a serious study of the problem and may be taken as a reliable witness, has told me on several occasions that it is better not to pay too much attention to existing social status: this will ensure selection on the basis of personal qualities from among all women equally, called as they are by the potential role of motherhood to assume responsibilities for which there is no equal elsewhere.[16]

By giving priority to education and culture, so that the individual can reflect on the meaning of development and the kind of contribution he or she can make towards it—only by this means can we open the way for the advent of the only effective power.

Towards another pattern of consumption

America, which, through the words of Fulbright, provided an illustration of the arrogance of power, remains one of the vantage points from which we can observe the emergence of the new values for which we are seeking. Although I cannot at all agree with Zbigniew Brzezinski[17] when he says: "I think America provides a vista to a future which most people aspire to . . .", I am nevertheless the first

---

[16] See in this connection "L'éducation comme moyen de corriger les inégalités nées de la division du travail traditionnelle entre les sexes" by Elzea Aventurin (paper submitted at the Research Symposium on "Women and Decision Making" organized in November 1975 by IILS and published in *Research Series* No. 23).

[17] Interview, 10 October 1977, *International Herald Tribune*.

to admit that, for anyone who knows America, there is undoubtedly something profoundly true in another statement by Brzezinski: "I think America does stir the imagination. I think America does challenge established verities."

Thus taking for example the market for consumer goods of all kinds, Hazel Henderson points out that, after having blown up demand to monstrous proportions thanks to the 20,000 million dollars spent on advertising every year, the companies are in many cases no longer able to deliver the goods required and the result has been what are now called demarketing campaigns.[18]

The electricity companies were the first to be affected owing to their importance in providing energy for other production processes as well as for home consumption. With the shortage and increasing cost of their primary fuel—coal, oil and natural gas—they were no longer able to meet both soaring production costs and consumer resistance to higher rates. The result was a reduction in a large number of electrical goods. The winter of 1973-4 saw the oil industry in a similar situation. The paradise of cheap petrol vanished like a dream and the most popular publicity slogan became: "Save petrol!"

At the present time certain categories of goods with a high energy component have already been banned. Using non-returnable containers for packaging is beginning to seem increasingly irresponsible; large, over-powerful cars are becoming difficult to sell.

Thus when President Carter launched his energy conservation programme and himself set an example by accepting the restrictions he imposed on his fellow citizens, even if the programme was not immediately successful, at least the ground had been prepared. In informed circles there is an awareness that the United States accounts for 6 per cent of the world population and consumes almost one-third of

---

[18] "More formally, we define demarketing *as that aspect of marketing that deals with discouraging customers in general or a certain class of customers in particular on either a temporary or permanent basis.*" Extract from an article by Philip Kotler and Sydney Levy: "Demarketing, yes, Demarketing" in *Harvard Business Review*, Nov.-Dec. 1971, p. 75.

Among the techniques used to discourage purchases may be mentioned: a reduction in advertising; a reduction in the time allotted to salesmen or their assignment to the sale of other products; the raising of prices or the elimination of discounts; an increase in the time and money needed to buy a product.

world oil production,[19] eight hundred million tons, over 400 million tons of which are imported, the equivalent of total Saudi Arabian production. If the annual growth in consumption continues at the present rate of 5 per cent, by 1985 the United States will have to import 575 million tons of oil. Today, in fact, Americans are burning 67 per cent more fuel than in 1973, the year of the first steep rise in the cost of oil. I should also like to remind the reader that at the last FAO World Conference (November-December 1977), the discussion of the report by Director-General Edouard Saouma revealed a sad situation which is causing concern to American Government circles themselves: the food wasted in the United States each year would be enough to feed 50 million people.

It is thus a matter of urgency to devise new aims for production and consequently a new pattern of consumption.

With this in mind, Hazel Henderson has shown that the companies which will be capable of adapting themselves to a period of "zero growth" will be those which supply the public sector, for example public transport and recycling, and those which cut down raw materials to a minimum, concentrating on durability rather than obsolescence. "Corporations may also have to be content with modest profit margins because the companies will have to internalize more of the social costs of production and consumption. And as energy for transportation becomes more realistically valued, over-centralized production by giant corporations will become less efficient than smaller regional and localized manufacturing serving de-centralized markets."[20]

If I have dwelt at some length on the American situation, it is in order to show that the supposedly affluent societies are already being confronted by the problem of poverty in power, and that it is not just for economic reasons that people are driving smaller cars, taking up bicycling or using public transport. No. There is also the satisfaction

---

[19] By comparison China, with at least 20 per cent of the world population, produced in 1976 about 3.3 per cent of the world annual volume of oil, some 88 million tons, of which a small quantity is even exported. Thus China consumes roughly one-tenth of the amount of oil consumed by the United States, with a population 3.8 times the size.

See also "Is energy conservation in the West detrimental to third world interests?", paper submitted by Ali A. Mazrui to the World Conference on "Alternatives to Growth, 77", 2-4 October 1977, The Woodlands, Texas.

[20] Hazel Henderson: "The Decline of Jonesism", *The Futurist*, October 1974, p. 220.

of growing one's own food and vegetables, the pleasure of physical exercise; above all, for those who are looking for it, there is the fulfilment which comes from the escape from the endless pursuit of goods.

A new meaning to the Wealth of Nations

François Perroux has already recognized the power of poverty in a paper which I find excellent and which has possibly been too quickly forgotten, presented by him on 11 October 1956 at La Tourette, under the auspices of "Economie et Humanisme". Taking 1948 as a base, Perroux points out that in that year the United States had a *per capita* income of 1525 dollars, the United Kingdom 777 dollars, the USSR 181 dollars, Czechoslovakia 345 dollars, Poland 190 dollars, Hungary 163 dollars and Bulgaria 113 dollars. He notes that, without allowing the accumulation of private wealth, the Soviet and Eastern bloc economies have become powerful. This, he feels, is not due merely to oppression. Another reason he evokes is the pooling of intelligence, a coalition of the poor which upsets the normal pattern of the market economy. Perroux concludes by noting that the power of poverty is certainly experienced by the poor, but also by the rich—astounded to find themselves confronted by poor people who have grown so powerful.

"The new power is gaining ground. The poor in various places have seen other poor people become powerful by *methods which are altogether different from traditional ways of making money*. A coalition of the poor against the former rich and the former masters is emerging throughout the world. After so many centuries have passed it is a response to the tacit coalition of the masters described by Adam Smith in his *Wealth of Nations*."

Perroux was writing in 1956 when little was known about China. Today we must throw it into the balance, if only to explain why Julius Nyerere has been so much inspired by it. The Arusha Declaration which proposed for Tanzania a system of self-reliance in all areas seems to me today the only sensible choice for Africa and many other Third World countries. In the first place, this is because although it is inspired by the Chinese experiment, *it is not a slavish copy of it*. It is new, Tanzanian, African. It relies not on constraints but on the enthusiasm of the people. Far from being arrogant, it is open to improvement.

Among the numerous countries I have visited, either privately or as an international official, Tanzania is one of the few where official policy clearly states:

"The development of a country is brought about by its people, not by money. Money, and the wealth it represents, is the result and not the basis of development. The four prerequisites of development are different; they are: People, Land, Good Policies, Good Leadership." [21]

What the Arusha Declaration has to teach us, not only in the modest booklet recently published in Dar-es-Salaam (The Arusha Declaration, *10 Years After*), but also in the course of even brief visits spent among the ordinary people of the country; what we learn from Nyerere is not pedantic or falsified statistics, not a marble palace or sonorous titles, but something which can only be the result of courage and clear-sightedness: failures recognized but progress nonetheless sustained; dignity not proclaimed by garrulous busy-bodies but shared by a whole people who bear its proud burden, in a country where the value of work has been restored, the peasant has been rehabilitated, and genuine development pursued without recourse to a security system based on physical or moral torture and without the institution of a "State religion" consisting of the idiotic personality cult of the leader including his most grotesque ideas and actions. But I must be careful or I shall be accused of laying it on too thick. And it is possible that I am exaggerating a little or at least being very idealistic. I make no apologies, however, since I am convinced that Tanzania knows how to recognize its own limitations, problems and contradictions. [22] Naturally the worshippers of worldly goods keep

[21] J. Nyerere: *Freedom and Socialism* (Dar-es-Salaam, 1968), p. 243.

[22] A statement by Nyerere confirms this: "We are under no illusions about the difficulty of the task we have undertaken. With few socialists we are trying to build socialism; with few people conscious of the basic requirements of democracy we are trying to achieve change by democratic means; with few technicians we are trying to effect a fundamental transformation of our economy. And with an educated élite whose whole teaching encouraged motives of individualistic advancement, we are trying to promote an egalitarian society."

their distance . . . and here it should be stressed that corruption is power confiscated by those who exercise it. Tanzanian friends with whom I have discussed the future of their country have always pointed out that every political leader is a social leader linked with a specific group by a contract which is no less valid for being, as often happens, a tacit one. He must work to achieve the aims jointly defined by the group which he represents, but he may also break the contract—and this is what constitutes corruption: the breaking of the social contract by a member of the élite, or a dominant group.

Weeding out corruption and tyranny

In a country where need is desperate and the urgency of action in the cause of justice and solidarity strikes us with a blinding flash of truth, the flagrant display of corruption which takes the form not only of the confiscation of power but also its corollary, the accumulation of goods which should belong to the community, can only lead to a profound divorce between the government and the people, especially when certain officials go so far as to provide their mistresses with the now famous trio of villa, car and bank account. One result is government instability perpetuated rather than remedied by successive *coups d'Etat.*

In my opinion we can draw some useful conclusions for my argument from certain events which have taken place recently in several different countries—in India where a former Prime Minister spent a night in prison on a charge of corruption,[23] in Syria where some very high officials have been forced to resign and appear in court, and so on.

---

[23] In the interests of truth, and in order to be completely fair, it should be admitted that the abandonment of the rule of law and the arbitrary way in which the professional classes and officials are treated in certain countries are distinctly conducive to corruption. Thus when for dubious or non-existent reasons, or merely because they offend the politicians of the day, perfectly honourable citizens, distinguished professional people, find themselves thrown into prison from one day to the next, without trial, deprived of resources, exiled and sometimes condemned to death, it is understandable why normally honest people are tempted to make provision for themselves and their families by engaging in some sometimes highly irregular operations. . . .

Respect for human rights is undoubtedly one of the best safeguards against the political uncertainty which encourages corruption, so rightly denounced.

Not long ago President Houari Boumedienne of Algeria denounced "parasitic behaviour and the pursuit of the easy life". He called for "priority for integrity" and stressed that there could be *"no revolution without morals"*.

Almost at the same time his opposite number in the Ivory Coast, President Houphouët-Boigny, said in a speech: "We must, above all, give serious attention to what has been called the disease of the century—corruption in all its forms." Abidjan too is now alive to a problem to which I have frequently referred throughout this book— the need to ensure that a country's resources are managed by its own people. Thus Albert Vanié-Bi-Tra is no longer just Minister of Labour, he has become: "Minister of Labour and the Ivorization of the Professional Classes" . . . while some people are apparently already becoming worried about the future of technical assistance. The appointment of a Minister of State, Matthieu Ekra, to supervise public corporations is a further sign of the great importance attached to a form of administration that is "different".

These examples, drawn from recent decisions or events related to local situations which may not be very well known, give further support, if such is needed, to my thesis on the need for a new pattern of development. In some cases, the situation is, in fact, so serious that the ordinary people have been shocked and shaken to the point that some have even gone so far as to succumb to the temptation of regretting the colonial period. Here we should recall the imprecations of folk minstrels like the famous N'Gon Koutou in Chad (who was later rehabilitated and proclaimed a national poet).

Chad at the time of the decline of the Tombalbaye regime could be described in two words: destitution and fascism. It might be more accurate to say absolute destitution and absolute fascism.

It was in this desert hell, torn with violence, that N'Gon Koutou, with almost suicidal courage, wrote a popular song which was enthusiastically taken up by all the peasants, and accompanied by the interminable chants of the women:

> "And you, agents of Tombalbaye, when will you go home to your villages, when will you make way for the Whites, when will they return so that at last we shall have enough to eat, at last we shall be able to breathe?"

The extravagant and ridiculous behaviour of which some Third
World leaders are guilty in the eyes of the world—and which is sometimes encouraged from outside—not only cuts them off from their
own people but leads to a revival in Europe and elsewhere of all the
movements which used to support and justify "cultural relativity"
and the relegation to an inferior status of cultures in whose name
colonization was seen as a civilizing mission. Books by Lévy-Brühl on
the "primitive mentality" are reappearing in bookshop windows and
Michel Sardou owes one of his greatest successes to a song which
celebrates "the happy days of the Colonies" . . . when in Colomb-
Béchar "I had masses of black servants and four girls in my bed".

This is by no means all. The increasing unemployment in industrialized
countries, accompanied as it is by violence and anarchy and nostalgia
for the past, has encouraged the birth of sinister foreign legions
peopled by new conquerors drunk on dreams of death and glory,
like the grotesque mercenaries who, thirsting for adventure, invaded
the Benin People's Republic on 16 January 1977.

In Chad the minstrel N'Gon Koutou is still alive, scrutinizing the
present with anxiety. Tombalbaye, despite his few redeeming moments
of lucidity and benevolence, has already paid with his life for the
tyranny he established. His case leads me to a question.

If remaining in power means not sleeping two nights running under
the same roof, or trembling each time a dog barks; if exercising power
means destroying others by fire and seeing oneself destroyed: what on
earth is the point of it all?

I believe that the answer to this tragic situation lies in setting up
a society of poverty where the rulers themselves set an example, for
people do follow the example of their leaders.

Building the co-operative republic

When I am asked how I envisage such a society, I am not afraid
to state my preference for a genuine "co-operative project" as Henri
Desroche[24] understands it. It is a vision of another kind of society

---

[24] See Henri Desroche: *Le projet coopératif* (Paris, Editions Economie et Humanisme,
Les Editions Ouvrières, 1976).

where a spirit of initiative, discipline and fellowship can bring the people together in one flourishing community.

I believe our thinking should be directed towards a co-operative system which is something more than a mere collection of isolated production and marketing projects co-existing with totally disorganized, exploitative, bureaucratic and militarist systems.

I think it is possible, especially in small countries, to design an overall plan which would combine all activities of production, trade and management at national level into a single co-operative project which would be a blueprint for society.

What the Rochdale pioneers and later Charles Gide failed to bequeath to their societies—and this was one of their major disappointments— was the *"co-operative republic"* which our own traditions make it easier for us to conceive.

It is thus our turn to explore along these lines. The "virtues" of co-operation as listed by Gide: a higher standard of living, cash payments, saving without hardship, doing away with parasites, combating the evils of drink, interesting women in social questions, providing inexpensive education for the people, making it easier for everyone to own property, building up collective property, establishing fair prices, abolishing capitalist profits, doing away with disputes— these virtues may appear naive to some people but they nevertheless remain the true foundation of any strategy for social control of needs. What we need is an overall co-operative framework where nothing can escape the ties of solidarity.

"Even inefficiently applied, even if it is utopian or mystical, even with an aura of magic", as the Brazilian Diva Benevides Pinho so rightly says, "co-operation is better than the rootlessness which results from the flight from the land and the appalling suffering of those who have broken all emotional ties with the old community without ever gaining a foothold in the new world: the vast mass of the unemployed, the unskilled, the homeless, the uncared for, 'those who will forever remain in transit on the road to nowhere'."[25]

The co-operative spirit emphasizes and gives priority to human relationships, not necessarily totally untroubled or free from conflict,

[25] *Revue des études coopératives*, Special issue, 1976.

but nevertheless implying the assumption of responsibility towards others and genuine solidarity both at work and in the organization of production.

This experience of direct relationships involving participation and personal commitment is an essential aspect of social life. It is also one of the choices open to society.

I foresee an objection: We cannot construct a model for community life by simply extrapolating from an ideal or from a few successful experiments based on that ideal. Social life is also made up of a whole series of constraints, burdens and ingrained habits which are partly due to the ossification, rigidity and increasing bureaucracy of social relationships. If we recognize this we are already on the way towards escaping from determinism. For the future development of society,[26] we must invent the co-operative republic to free us from centralized State bureaucracy, that often arbitrary, always rigid, cold and cynical Leviathan.

It is a possible blueprint for development which may conceivably galvanize the energy of peoples who, as Schumacher suggests, will thus be choosing an economic model which best suits *themselves*.

Obviously in a republic or society of this kind we will have to work out other forms of "hierarchy".

"In order to do great things", said Montesquieu, "it is not necessary to be above men, it is necessary to be with them."

At the same time it should always be remembered that the duty of freedom is not incompatible with *social discipline*. Not only are they both essential, but in fact each justifies the other, especially if the targets for development, collectively defined, are at the same time the yardstick for individual behaviour.

In a society based on participation, the division between management and executive functions, for example, would tend to be reduced.

In order that it is not always the same people who have to carry out the unpleasant tasks, it might be possible to introduce a system of rotation of jobs.

[26] I should like to draw attention to the World Social Prospects Study Association, set up in Geneva on the occasion of the World Symposium on the Social Implications of a New International Economic Order (International Institute for Labour Studies, 19-23 January 1976).

Examples already exist of urban districts where garbage is collected in turn by different teams, all of whom are eligible for local government.

Roger Garaudy, in his project "Hope", suggests another kind of rotation: "In order to avoid giving permanence to the delegation of power and the professionalization of politics, the principle of rotation should be strictly applied: no-one should be re-eligible twice running for public assemblies. Moreover, if the delegates do not represent an electoral district but a working, consumer or cultural unit, it is perfectly possible that the delegate of the unit need not always be the same, but could be chosen for each session of the congress and workers' councils in the light of the nature of the problems on the agenda of that session. Far from being utopian, this principle has been expressly embodied in the latest Yugoslav constitution."

When, to the general surprise of all, Muammar El Qaddafi questions the whole institution of domestic servants, I for my part see the beginnings of a society of poverty based on equally shared responsibility in every sphere.

As J. P. N'Diaye says in *Monde noir et Destin politique*, "one feels that the heart of the problem still remains that of finding a sense of direction, drawing up an *inner code* which will govern our future destiny and be the vital impulse of all our creation".

The greatest benefit which a society of poverty would provide seems to me to be the principle of the ontological equality of human beings and the great variety of their formal differences.

Ontological equality is always threatened by the cultural relativity which stems from the arrogance of money. Nor is it any use seeking to affirm this equality of being by means of criteria drawn from commercial capitalism which lay down the basis for a society of *apartheid* by calling for a property qualification for suffrage. Franz Fanon has already warned the "damned of the earth": "No, we do not want to overtake anyone. But we want to go on walking all the time, night and day, in company with our fellow men, all our fellow men."

Once wealth becomes collective and poverty is shared, it seems to me that ontological equality will have a better chance of taking root. Only then will the formal differences cause the whole to bear fruit because they are based on human beings, and all their varied manifestations, on more immediate communication, a deeper sense of fellowship.[27]

It is a fact that the poor—not the destitute—set us an inspiring example by their simplicity, hard work, generosity and not least by their realism.

It is they who in Brazil have invented the "mutiaro" and in Haiti the "coumbite" to give concrete expression to the idea of working together collectively for the good of all, because "helping one another is the friendship of the poor". We must organize poverty, believe in it, establish it on the basis of collective rights which give us freedom and liberate the spirit of fellowship—the only force, the only power which will surely bring us together. "And we shall assemble all those lords of the morning dew, the great community of the tillers of the soil, to clear destitution from the land and sow the seeds of a new life."

[27] It is interesting to note that a similar message was proclaimed as early as 1959 by the Frenchman L.-J. Lebret who referred to frugality where I have used the term poverty. He said in a short book, *Pour une civilisation solidaire* (Paris, Editions Ouvrières, 1963), p. 46: "The ideal of wealth and especially wealth devoted to maximum comfort, is not the optimum ideal for humanity . . . if destitution, in other words life below the level of subsistence and dignity, is an evil to be combated, *frugality*, or need reduced to the requirements of a life of dignity, is a value which can confer on peoples who are less rich a superiority over nations which care above all for ease and comfort.

"In addition, *frugality* ensures that, as *per capita* production increases, more resources can be devoted to communal facilities for both cultural and spiritual activities."

CHAPTER V

For a Solidarity Contract

" . . . A cut is made in the arm of each party to the contract who then touches the blood of the other with his lips . . . The two men become more than friends; they regard each other as brothers."

  Blood Covenant ceremony among the Kikuyu.

"Give me a fulcrum and I'll lift the world."

  (Archimedes)

In the depth of the crisis confronting our societies, the daunting problems facing us, there is still hope.

Manuel, the hero of *Gouverneurs de la rosée*[1] *(Lords of the Morning Dew)*, found the spring which would restore his community to life. He fell victim to jealousy and hate, but he left this testament: ". . . reconciliation, reconciliation so that life can start again, and the sun rise on the dew-covered earth". And in fact, an immense "coumbite", the combined efforts of all the people, day after day, caused the water to gush forth. *Solidarity had triumphed.*

And this remains our opportunity and our hope today. Through solidarity the poor can get together to enhance the welfare of all.

But how can this be organized? How can poverty in power lead us to a fuller participation of all the people in our collective life, enriched by each individual's special contribution?

I say that this can be done through a *Solidarity Contract*, an idea which in my view should be included in the demand for a New International Order which will demonstrate the power of poverty.

---

[1] See the introductory quotation on page 90.

"We, the peoples of the United Nations"
or the forgotten majority

Since the fate of mankind is at stake—"the only battle worth fighting"—we must take up a challenge commensurate with the stakes. We must recognize, with Aurelio Peccei, that a new ethic is needed to bring about the truly "human revolution"—the revolution in our own minds.[2] It was the same concern that led Pope Paul VI, speaking to representatives of non-Christian religions, to say that: "Man must meet man; the nations must meet as brothers. . . . In this mutual understanding and friendship, in this sacred communion, we must start to work together to build the common future of mankind."[3]

Such an appeal may give the impression that solidarity between nations is of the same nature, and just as easy to achieve, as solidarity between related groups. But the nature of the relationships, the scale of the problems and the means of communication and dialogue are quite different and call for specific institutional and legal forms. However, despite the inevitable conflicts and trials of strength, international relations must be guided by a principle of solidarity, a willingness to negotiate which, in the last analysis, must take precedence over relations based on pure violence.

Hitherto, however, the mainspring of the world in which we live has been not a shared sense of solidarity but a dialectic in which domination and subjection—fed with egoism and resentment—predominate over the positive and dynamic factors of progress. In these circumstances we may well ask, what do they amount to, these "peoples of the United Nations" whose high-minded alliance was meant to guarantee world peace? Who are these peoples? The "marginals", the unemployed, the sick, the handicapped—all those who are described as the "non-integrated"?

Unfortunately, these are not the ones we are thinking of when we speak of "We, the peoples of the United Nations". But this forgotten majority, these people left by the wayside, on the "fringe", unemployed, sick, justly demand the right to live. And it is a matter of urgency to

[2] A. Peccei: *La qualité humaine* (Paris, Stock, 1976).

[3] Address to the representatives of non-Christian religions, 3 December 1964, AAS 57 (1965).

meet this legitimate claim by hastening the advent of a new international order.

In the eyes of many, the "order" in which we live today is

—an "order" without dialogue, a universe in which the rulers conduct a soliloquy to which, for centuries, we have been accustomed to listen passively;

—an "order" based on privilege whose structure enables a minority to dictate laws and rules of conduct to the majority;

—an "order" in which, most of the time, the principles of justice, equity and solidarity give way to considerations of power and profit.

Today these privileges are clearly being challenged.[4] And if there is no response to the demands which are being voiced, the inevitable outcome will be the revolution predicted by Mirabeau: "Callous egoists who imagine that these convulsions of despair will pass over the more quickly the more violent they are, are you so certain that so many who have no bread will quietly let you enjoy all those numerous and refined dishes which you have refused to give up? No, you will perish!"

The danger, in fact, lies mainly in the type of international relations engendered by the imperial system that is now contested, which has given rise to institutions in which unity is imposed from outside. Specialists in German company law contrast the type of institution known as "Herrschaft", based on domination, and the "Genossenschaft", whose unity is constituted democratically.

A keener perception of existing distortion and injustice has led to certain awakenings, to certain questions being asked. The struggle and resistance of the hungry peoples have shaken the edifice. We cannot but rejoice to see that efforts carried on within the United Nations have recently led to two events of the first importance:

—the Declaration and Programme of Action on the establishment of a new international economic order, adopted by the General Assembly at its sixth Special Session on 1 May 1974; and

—the Charter of the Economic Rights and Duties of States, adopted

---

[4] See E. Kodjo: "Justice and equity must gradually make way for a contractual solidarity resulting from a new attitude, which agrees that vertical, i.e. global, solutions shall be found for vertical problems (poverty wherever it may be, distribution, security)." Algiers, October 1976.

at the 29th regular session on 12 December 1974, indissolubly associated with the name of the former Mexican President, Luis Echeverría.

A new order that brings freedom

These texts along with some others[5] reflect the will, expressed on numerous occasions by a large number of countries and peoples, to seek to introduce a new equilibrium and a new type of development based on a new approach to relations among States, among peoples and among men. We must grasp the opportunity offered by this new approach to recast development models, by giving social phenomena the importance that should always have been theirs.

But the difficulties of such a change must not be underestimated. On the contrary, we must continually emphasize how much better it is to negotiate calmly and deliberately, between partners, in a long-term perspective, than to act hastily, under compulsion, as events often force us to do. What we need is a plan for the future—and it must be a *social* plan. The quest for a just international order calls for the adoption and acceptance by all members of the international community of principles which guarantee its legitimacy and, to a greater extent than in the past, the peoples of the Third World must share in defining those principles.

In the eyes of these peoples, one of the essential meanings of a New International Order, and one which I should like to stress, is: *the liberation of peoples*. The Algerian national Charter reminds us of this: "The concept of development cannot be dissociated from that of economic liberation." Liberation: because the existing "order", which we condemn, constitutes a historic mutilation or "alienation", in Adam Schaff's sense of a borrowed culture, a borrowed personality.

The peoples of the Third World, armed with their inalienable right to liberation, are determined to participate on an equal footing in a human condition that is "experienced in common and shared together", as is warranted by man's common destiny. They want co-operation; but first of all they want justice. But the times in

---

[5] The Cocoyoc Declaration adopted at the UNEP/UNCTAD Symposium on Patterns of Resource Use, Environment and Development Strategies, Mexico, 10-12 October 1974.

which we live are dangerous for man's spirit. The confusion of terms and intentions may wreck the most noble undertakings.

We should therefore keep in mind that an appeal for solidarity is not in itself enough to establish universal standards of behaviour or models that can be systematically applied. We, the peoples of the Third World, have suffered too much from a thousand ambiguities not to be mistrustful of vague and generous-sounding concepts: the ambiguities of charity and of fraternity, the ambiguities even of freedom and of culture. We cannot therefore agree to take as our watchword an ambiguous "solidarity" which is merely a pretext for the maintenance of domination and a system of built-in injustice under the guise of "benevolence". I have often heard trade unionists, workers and other militants say, very rightly, that "The solidarity of the horse and the rider is not our kind of solidarity, and we want nothing of it".

It is evident, however, that the importance of solidarity is being more and more widely recognized. Leonid Brezhnev, for example, was thinking in terms of solidarity when he took the initiative—of capital importance—of launching the Conference on Security and Co-operation in Europe, which resulted in the Helsinki Declaration, all the consequences of which for the daily life of the peoples have not yet been revealed. The Helsinki Declaration, which "destabilizes" the permanent ideological tension, also affects other essential fields, such as economic and social development, culture and the movement of men and ideas. It thus lays the foundations of a veritable "contract of co-existence" between peoples living under different political systems. Whatever momentary difficulties may arise—and, in fact, precisely because of the public controversies we are witnessing—the results of the Conference on Security and Co-operation in Europe will, for a long time to come, affect the structure and relations not only of the States directly concerned, but also of all the others associated with them in this global adventure which is, in the last analysis, a matter for all mankind.

Thus, ever since the welcome initiative of Pierre Mendès-France launched his country on a policy of decolonization, past history and present circumstances have impelled the Paris government towards an active policy of co-operation. On the occasion of Djibouti's accession to independence in June 1977, and again during his official visit to the Ivory Coast in January 1978, Mr. Valéry Giscard d'Estaing referred to the developments we have noted here and called for a pact of solidarity between Europe and Africa. Previously, Lionel Jospin and Jacques Delors of the French Socialist Party had put forward the idea of a "co-development contract".

These generous and relevant ideas deserve recognition. Once again, however, we must not forget that the colonial mentality is far from dead and that no one in the Third World wants to prolong its existence on the basis of woolly phrases. In particular, the current ferment in southern Africa, where racial and racist contempt are leading to a policy of deliberate genocide, cannot be left out of the picture. How can we, in the West or elsewhere, pretend to overlook the fact—so frequently stressed by Diallo Telli, Secretary-General of the Organization of African Unity—that any open or surreptitious complicity with the protagonists of so vast a tragedy, involving incalculable risks for the world as a whole, is totally incompatible with an ethic of solidarity?

It does credit to the courage of Andrew Young, United States Ambassador, that he has grasped this fact, which imposes on all of us the obligation to speak out clearly and to avoid, in the phrase of Pierre Waline (former vice-chairman of the ILO Governing Body) the "evil influence of misleading language".

I should like, therefore, to try once again to explain what I mean by the "solidarity contract" and suggest what its conditions and areas of application might be, as I set them out, in broad outline, in January 1976 at the World Symposium on the Social Implications of a New International Economic order.

What sort of solidarity?

Serious study and research should enable us to get a clearer idea of this concept in the new context and in relation to the specific needs which concern us here. Starting from "Herrschaft"—characterized by domination—and "Genossenschaft"—based on co-operation— we can distinguish two concepts of solidarity:

—mechanical solidarity, based on resemblance, which is the sheep-like attachment of the individual to the group; and

—organic solidarity, based on differences, which is the response to the creative aspirations of each and to the genuine needs of all, and is the real objective of our search.

Every passing day gives us the opportunity to measure our indifference or our sensitivity to this organic solidarity.

We are constantly being reminded of it by the radio, television, newspapers:

—two giant aircraft collide—800 dead;

—earthquakes in Turkey, Romania, Guatemala—thousands of dead and homeless;

—floods, mountain disasters, road accidents—deaths and more deaths. . . .

And we are in the land of the living.

A few good Samaritans try to help the traveller fallen among thieves, tortured and left for dead.

Their sense of solidarity makes us feel guilty. But we should go a bit further than worrying, as we sit comfortably in our armchairs, about being condemned for "failure to assist persons in danger".

The whole world should and can live in organic solidarity. We can make this happen by opening our eyes to the unceasing disasters that pile up thousands of corpses for which we are all jointly responsible.[6]

If we realize that the failure to satisfy basic needs constitutes, in the short or the long run, a real calamity for a people which, like any other calamity, calls for solidarity, we can, then, imagine a situation in which a given Third World country could itself define precise social objectives in a particular sector, would itself indicate the basic requirements that ought to be met within a given time-limit if those objectives are to be attained, and the ways and means of achieving them, drawing up, as it were, a set of instructions for meeting social needs.

The resources to be mobilized would be primarily internal, but they

---

[6] P.-M. Henry: "The ultimate consequences of total solidarity among human beings all over the world has not yet been carefully estimated either in the East or in the West, either by the rich or by the poor nations. Nobody has yet thought out in all its economic and political implications what a genuine guarantee that everybody shall have enough to live on, at a level enabling them to progress and think for themselves, would mean in terms of food, housing, education and health." (*La force des faibles*, Paris, Editions Entente, 1975.)

would also include reliance on the country's participation in international economic, commercial, political and cultural co-operation. Such a system would enable an industrialized country, another Third World country or an international organization to offer its contribution to the implementation of various projects by making available its transferable experience, technical or financial resources, or temporary staff sent to work directly on the spot.

One can imagine other situations in which an industrialized country, in order to meet some essential need—for water, energy, manpower or better social relations—has to seek, on a basis of complementarity, the solidarity of a Third World country or of another industrialized country.

Thus contracts for a technological exchange between two States or for a regional rural development plan can only be solidarity contracts if they meet the following conditions:

—satisfaction of the basic needs of the populations covered by the agreement; and

—the adoption of the principle of negotiation and action in concert without any form of commercial or financial dependence.

As Amadou-Mahtar M'Bow, Director-General of UNESCO, has so wisely put it, the underlying objective is to "get beyond the sterile, unstable and dangerous system of relations based on power and exploitation",[7] and thus to bring about a new type of international relations. This proves that solidarity can no longer be merely a general, ambiguous principle, quickly forgotten. It must become a genuine contract linking individuals and communities who have previously defined clear and noble objectives based on a human condition experienced in common and shared together.

It is not the purpose of this work to analyse the forms and nature of new international relations needed to establish the new order so much talked of today. It is important, however, to emphasize in passing the necessity for structural reforms in the relations between nation-

[7] Message to the World Symposium on the Social Implications of a New International Economic Order (Geneva, January 1976). Mr. M'Bow also said, "The drive for development and the introduction of a new international economic order are henceforth inseparable: together they constitute a global undertaking which is the work of man in the service of man."

States and the national sovereignties which they claim. As Belaïd Abdesselam, Algerian Minister of Industry, said at the RIO Project Symposium held in Algiers in October 1976, "While it is true that the development of each country depends essentially and primarily on the efforts of its own people, it is none the less true that these efforts need to be complemented and supported by equitable international relations purged of all forms of domination and exploitation." But such a change in international power structures will only be real and durable if it is based on new forms of national development.

That is why I wish to stress once more the need to mobilize internal resources. For "there is no development that is not *self*-development . . . and the struggle for development which calls forth and enhances the cultural virtues of each people must be based, in the first place, on the living sources of that culture, i.e. on the masses of the people" (J. Ki-Zerbo).

In the effort for internal mobilization, qualified professionals have an important role to play. If—deliberately or not—they are lacking in the spirit and practice of national solidarity, this lack must be filled by "outside technical assistants". If a local doctor, teacher or agronomist insists on working in the town, if he scorns the countryside and turns up his nose at a job in the backwoods, there is nothing surprising in the fact that a "technical assistant", who is willing to work anywhere he is needed, must be called in to take his place. And often, of course, we are filled with admiration for their generous-hearted and brotherly work. . . . On the other hand, however, it sometimes happens that these co-operators are tempted by a shallow curiosity, political interventionism—rightwing or leftwing—by adventure, by some secret sideline or by a low form of anthropology. . . .[8]

But what can we do if we have ourselves failed to understand where our duty lies and the fact that our long-term interests require that we

[8] Certain industrialized countries have adopted a system of National Service Volunteers who are tending to replace the former co-operators. These are young conscripts who, instead of military service, do a form of civilian service which consists of accepting a contract for technical co-operation work. This practice has a number of drawbacks which do serious damage to the very principle of co-operation.

During the seventies, Henri Bandolo devoted one of his Sunday programmes of criticism, "Dominique", on Radio Yaoundé to certain leisure activities of the national service volunteers—greatly upsetting public opinion and the authorities.

rely on our own resources for the solidarity that is now being offered from outside?

The men who succeed in making a useful contribution in an "underdeveloped" society are those who have chosen poverty, meaning not only the detachment from material goods, but also the need to learn from others the art of living, of loving, of possessing what it takes to be a real human being: goodness, courage, real brotherliness, as the daughters of Shango say in Bahia. Here we are a long way from the sense of nothingness we feel when, with the eyes of France Pastorelli, we encounter certain people, moral invertebrates who, when reduced to their basic reality, "in circumstances which strip them of the varnish they owe to civilization and education, look like nothing but useless dummies, inert, pitiful and ugly, like tortoises without their shells".[9] Unfortunately, as François de Negroni shows us, co-operation provides some such examples.[10]

Solidarity among whom?

Defined by the criteria of truth and service and thus safe from all ambiguity, solidarity can manifest itself at different levels. We must, however, answer a question that is often asked: "Solidarity among whom?" For the contract that we envisage is not an arbitrary encounter of free agents, but the "common and responsible creation of genuine human progress".[11] And since there can be no creation without creators, such a contract presupposes *partners* "clearly identified as such and assured of the economic, political and cultural conditions for exercising the responsibility with which they are invested".

The international community which for a long time consisted solely of States has been gradually making room for private individuals. Thus it is the peoples in their national structures, their public and private organizations and the individuals who compose them which

[9] F. Pastorelli: *Servitude et grandeur de la maladie* (Paris, Editions du Cerf, 1968).

[10] François de Negroni: *Les colonies de vacances* (Paris, Editions Hallier, 1977).

[11] Cardinal B. Gantin: Statement to the Round Table on the occasion of the 10th anniversary of the Encyclical "Populorum Progressio", IILS, 1977. Published in *Progrès des peuples et solidarité mondiale* (Geneva, IILS, 1977), pp. 43-46.

are all equally involved. The Solidarity Contract is a matter for all men and all communities. We must *recognize* ourselves as we are, all of us, each with some weakness, each with some need to be met either at the personal, national or international level. And it may be useful here to recall what we said at the beginning of this chapter: "large-scale" solidarity among national groups has neither the same structure, the same nature nor the same laws as in the case of individual relationships.

It is, in fact, commonly held that, when dealing with international economic and political problems, it is primarily the attitude of the nation-State that must be taken into consideration. While the essential dimension of the problem of "international" solidarity cannot, of course, be overlooked, I would like to stress here the fact that we must not attach sole or always primary importance to official policy. It is among the peoples themselves and the often down-trodden masses that we must seek the driving force and political dynamism required to bring forth the effective will to solidarity and to transform it into politically recognized projects and contracts.

One example of internal solidarity is the praiseworthy concern that has recently appeared in several countries to heighten the prestige of manual work by paying higher, more respectable, wages for this type of activity. But is this the right way of seeing the problem? Should manual work be revalued by better pay? Or should man's work be given greater value by seeking a more equitable synthesis between the intellectual element and the muscular? There should not be two categories of men: the rich who need to engage in sport to keep their bodies in trim, and the poor who are forced to accept the enslavement of their minds because their bodies are far too tired for the effort of thought and self-renewal.

If manual work could become a part of the inventive effort and of technological progress, these two inalienable facets of the creative power of each individual would be brought into balance.

Working with the hands and with the mind: a synthesis in the service of man and of social progress. The recognition of their complementarity would perhaps lead on to other beneficial advances in everything relating to education, employment, health and the quality of life. And if this awareness becomes generalized, a new internal solidarity will be born in each country and will acquire a contractual status.

Once again at the national level, and in line with the proposals for a "Co-operative Republic", the solidarity contract can be applied in different situations: between the rulers or technicians and the masses, between regions, between social groups, and so forth.

It is obvious that if, at the national level, our countries relied in the first place on themselves for development, international co-operation would have a solid foundation, giving it substance and effectiveness. And in return, the philosophy of the new order would gradually impose new political and social orientations and would abolish privileges.

May I take this opportunity to stress a concept of the first importance: the *solidarity of the poor*? This is what I. Jazaïry calls "the fighting solidarity of the third-world countries". [12] It is this that enables them to work out a concerted stand on clear objectives and to plan jointly a global strategy in conformity with the rights of peoples and at the same time set up complementary development machinery. The Third World countries first demonstrated their awareness of their common struggle at the time of the preparations for the first session of the United Nations Conference on Trade and Development in 1964, but it was unquestionably at the Fourth Summit Conference of the Non-Aligned Countries in Algiers in September 1973 that it was best displayed. When, on that occasion, President Houari Boumedienne called for a new world economic order and expressed the hope that its advent would bring "victory over poverty, disease and insecurity", it was one and the same issue that was at stake: the refusal, by solidarity, of structures imposed through unilaterally installed machinery. The new positions won by the OPEC countries by determining the price of oil demonstrates the strength of such solidarity. Already it is providing a model for other alliances. Thus, thanks to their awareness of this fighting solidarity, the Third World countries will succeed in creating an instrument capable of promoting their liberation. Indeed, we cannot be satisfied with an "ethic of sentiments", which may lead to

---

[12] I. Jazaïry: *Le concept de solidarité internationale pour le développement* (Geneva, IILS, 1977).

a ghastly pact obliging us to swallow our hunger. Quite to the contrary, our purpose is to strive for higher things and find a direction that will integrate the protest function by establishing the rules of the game in the framework of a structure that takes account of *mutual interests.* "Protest has a stimulating rôle to play since it serves to prevent solidarity, once regained, from becoming mired in mere accommodation or compromises in the name of social peace which may in some cases be more a reflection of the solidarity of powerful interests than a guarantee of, or a means of promoting, basic human rights."[13]

But solidarity should not be confined merely to economics. Applied in all fields and operated at different levels, it will lead to a rapid expansion of horizontal relations, thus multiplying the possibilities for a new form of international co-operation.

Solidarity, therefore, being of universal application, also has a twofold nature. On the one hand, it may be regarded as a mere option: the right to take part in economic co-operation irrespective of all differences between political, economic and social systems; the right to form producers' associations and to take part in sub-regional and interrregional co-operation. On the other hand, it may be formulated in more imperative terms and regarded as a duty imposing different obligations on the various partners in the Solidarity Contract.

A prerequisite: respect for the partner

The conditions for all genuine co-operation and for the framing and implementation of any solidarity contract are well known. They may be summed up thus: respect for the partner, for his person, his views and his culture.

This is because we owe to ourselves the respect which is the basis of all human relations, because "the humiliation of man by man is contrary to the will of God" and because there is no future where-ever instinct has supplanted reason. But solidarity becomes reasonable when it is faithfully negotiated and if it forms part of a contract of conduct, of life and of creation.

13 Cf. "Justice, contestation et solidarité" by Carlos Josaphat Pinto de Oliveira, in *La justice,* conference papers (Fribourg, Editions Universitaires, 1977).

To the respect for culture I would add the respect for hospitality, because abuse of hospitality is always an offence against solidarity.

Poverty goes hand in hand with hospitality. If, as Saint Augustine says, "he who has more than he needs possesses the goods of others", it is clear that the philosophy and practice of sharing is characteristic above all of those for whom life has never had the meaning of the selfish amassment of property. But the tourist or co-operator who, welcomed in a village of simple people, takes advantage of and abuses their hospitality, is a traitor to the concept of hospitality. Thus the films that are shown here and there about voodoo or female circumcision cannot fail to arouse our legitimate apprehensions. They cater to a form of publicity which has nothing to do with solidarity. The taste for sensational ethnological curiosities ministers to the taste for violence and arouses contempt. This is not the way to prepare oneself to negotiate a solidarity contract because the final result is, through lack of understanding and ethnocentrism, to create division among men. Let us be precise. In speaking of films about female circumcision I am referring specifically to the campaign recently launched by *"Terre des Hommes"*[14] against the mutilation of young girls of marriageable age practised in certain countries of Africa and the Near East. The purpose of the campaign is doubtless wholly admirable; but certain of the methods used were utterly contemptible.

Eight o'clock in the evening on 4 May 1977: the time for the newsreel on the second French television channel. We listen with interest to Jean-Pierre Elkabach speaking about the Polisario's attack on Zouerate in Mauritania in which a French doctor and his wife were killed. There are commentaries, reactions. And then, almost without transition we are shown a sequence presented by a *"Terre des Hommes"* doctor where we see black men in an African country dancing around the horrible ceremonies of female circumcision.

I hasten to state that I am personally opposed to this custom, not through conventional squeamishness, but because respect for cultures and traditions cannot run counter to respect for the integrity of the human person.´

[14] A non-governmental organization for assistance to suffering children, with Headquarters at Lausanne, Switzerland. "Terre des Hommes" medical work is usually very valuable, but its publicity methods are not always well advised.

Having said this, I maintain that the *Terre des Hommes* doctor who presented the television sequence in question cannot have been unaware that he was failing to observe the code of conduct of his mission and thereby abusing the hospitality of the country that had received him. In what conditions was such a film made? It is our moral duty to raise that question.

In my view, one thing is certain: a televised sequence in a European newsreel is neither the time nor the place to tackle seriously the question of female circumcision in Africa or elsewhere. There are situations and practices which public opinion, however great the indignation aroused, cannot change because they fall within an area where outside intervention has no hold: that of basic social structures. In this realm, sensationalism may run counter to effectiveness, thus preventing or long delaying change which is nevertheless desirable.

That is to say that the presentation of the same film might have been acceptable if it had been accompanied by a careful analysis defusing merely skin-deep reactions and presented to a public genuinely interested in the subject, capable of seeing how the desired evolution might be brought about and wanting to show an intelligent and active solidarity. If that had been done, the peasant of the Aveyron or elsewhere to whom, among others, the television news is addressed would have gained a clearer view of the problem and would certainly have abstained from any hasty judgment which does not always promote the mutual understanding and respect which one people owes to another.

If I mention this incident and my reaction to it—which I reported to the press (see *Le Monde* of 11 May 1977)—it is in order to point out that, by employing other methods, we may have a better chance of reaching those who are really in a position to bring about change. These are, in the first place, the populations concerned. There is no doubt that if we were told more about the work of community development groups which comprise women, young workers and nurses of the countries concerned, this would do far more than a campaign launched in Lausanne by *"Terre des Hommes"* and more than all the resolutions passed by all the international organizations combined.

The role of world opinion—in which I believe—is to back the authentic movement of the peoples themselves and not to act as a substitute for it.

To do otherwise is to remain bogged down in old-fashioned forms of technical assistance and to encourage the snap judgments which provide a basis for all those forms of racism that we still deplore; it is to forget that to make a success of co-operation in the world of today, we must first of all take seriously and abide *strictly* by the dictum of Césaire which sums up my own argument as well as the profound feelings of the peoples of the Third World: "We must understand that henceforth we cannot allow anyone, even our best friend, to act as our champions. . . . It is time for us to prove ourselves."[15]

Contractual procedure

It is for this reason that negotiation among partners has become a categorical imperative. Such negotiation should aim at determining clear objectives, stages and conditions and should always be based on a profound sense of human fellowship.

Just as the application by States of international labour standards is the subject of periodical evaluation, so it is to be expected that solidarity contracts will only deserve the name when it has been demonstrated that they conform in practice to a number of rigorous criteria aligned on the principles which form the basis of a new international order. We must be careful to avoid describing as a "solidarity contract" any co-operation agreement up-dated to suit contemporary tastes! One of the original features of the Solidarity Contract is the adoption of a control and evaluation procedure based on principles that are no longer merely economic, but which take account of all the social dimensions of man.

Before the contract, the partners will consent to be guided by general considerations such as:

—the identification of global objectives designed to facilitate the introduction of an international order based on solidarity;

—the identification, through the negotiation process of immediate objectives related to the satisfaction of specific basic needs;

—the evaluation of the possibilities for pooling the resources required for the implementation of a given project.

[15] Aimé Césaire: *Lettre à Maurice Thorez* (Paris, Présence africaine, 1956).

During the execution of the contract, the same partners will adopt a suitable procedure enabling them to evaluate the progress made towards the goals, to foresee the next stages of the project, to reformulate objectives in the light of realities, in a word, to remain masters of the situation and control the future. If it is found that the operation no longer corresponds to the objectives, the contract should be revised. The really specific feature of the Solidarity Contract is the area to which it applies and the objectives it aims at: society, reconstituted as a living tissue.

After the completion of the contract, the partners will be bent on evaluating the results in the light of the objectives aimed at. The implications of a Solidarity Contract go beyond the mere consideration of the rights and duties resulting from it. The notions of economic advantage and of mutual benefit, considered as mere tools of negotiation, should take second place as compared with standards of justice and equity.

This evaluation should take account of different situations and lead to meaningful comparisons. Thus calculations in terms of money often mask the reality of the work done and prevent a correct appreciation of the economic and social utility of a project. What, for example, would the railway linking Tanzania and Zambia have cost if the project had had to be valued at current international prices?

But even if we confine ourselves to the financial evaluation of the obligations of the parties concerned in a Solidarity Contract, we can sometimes discern situations of injustice which give the lie to certain forms of ostensible beneficence.

In this connection, Appendix III contains a table of the financial transfers to the developing countries from the OECD countries. These transfers are well below those which take place in the opposite direction. This can be seen from calculations made by UNCTAD, which estimates at US$ 46,300 million the flow of aid from the United States, Canada and the United Kingdom to the Third World between 1960 and 1972. During the same period, the return flow of repayments, interest, profits and the contributions of technicians who migrated from the Third World into these three countries—the so-called "brain drain"—amounted to US$ 50,900 million: thus, despite aid, or perhaps as a result of it, the Third World had a negative balance of

US$ 4600 million during those 12 years. This calculation vividly illustrates the profound inequalities that must be corrected by new contractual structures. In the light of it we understand why the Algerian Jazaïry claims for the men and women of the Third World "the simple right to enjoy the surplus-value of their labour".

Since, as we have pointed out, solidarity is a factor of togetherness, it should display itself in all aspects of social life. This is why the specific content of each solidarity contract should be defined in terms of *social development*, having as its fundamental and immediate objectives the satisfaction of basic needs. This objective in itself determines the priority field of action of this type of contract. The first stage must therefore be to draw up a list of the most destitute, most compelling situations in which large numbers of individuals, communities or regions find themselves, with a view to identifying the priority areas in which the negotiation of solidarity contracts is a necessity.

Trade unions are indispensable—but what sort of unions?

It follows from this that, among the partners in a Solidarity Contract aimed at social development, a leading position must be reserved for all those groupings which help us to get a clearer view of the concerns, interests and needs of the poorest groups in the population. Among such groupings, I should like to assign a special place to trade union and professional organizations—*provided that they are not a shelter for selfish privilege at the expense of a destitute majority.*

The international covenant on economic, social and cultural rights adopted by the United Nations General Assembly in 1966 specifically affirms "the right of everyone to form trade unions and to join the trade union of his choice, subject only to the rules of the organization concerned, for the promotion and protection of his economic and social interests".[16]

Despite this affirmation, there are not many developing countries in which trade unions exist in all branches of the economy. And where

---

[16] International Covenant on Economic, Social and Cultural Rights, Resolution 2200 (XXI), of 16 December 1966, Article 8, paragraph 1, sub-paragraph (a).

they do exist they seldom have the strength, independence and representativeness necessary to be really effective instruments of participation by all workers in the establishment of a new international economic order.

In 1972, Wilfred Jenks, the Director-General of the International Labour Office, in his report to the International Labour Conference, highlighted that question and set targets for the ILO in this field: "Too often they are regarded by governments as instruments of political support or as sources of political danger. Too often their membership, and consequently their action, is restricted to a relatively small group of workers in the modern industrial sector."[17]

Thus the first target is to promote the creation and development of workers' organizations where they do not already exist. The agricultural sector is of particular relevance here. While, in the world as a whole, two out of three persons belong to the rural sector, this proportion is even greater in the developing countries. Since we know that, from the trade union standpoint, rural areas are less well organized than the towns, we can gain some idea of the magnitude of the task. The international Labour Conference has adopted a convention and a recommendation on rural workers' organizations and their role in economic and social development,[18] the essential aim of which is to propose internal measures—in the fields of legislation, finance, information and education—and to encourage their application.

It is for the trade union organizations to encourage the creation of co-operatives and other institutions for helping the peasants and craftsmen, who often live in extreme poverty, to increase their output, to market their products and thus to increase their income. Trade unions also have an irreplaceable part to play in social education, in population control and in the protection of the environment. In many countries, they may be decisive factors in improving social

[17] International Labour Conference, 57th session, *Technology for Freedom: Man in his Environment; the ILO Contribution*, Report by the Director General, Part I (Geneva, ILO, 1972), p. 52.

[18] International Labour Conference, 59th session, *Organization of Rural Workers and their Role in Economic and Social Development*. Report IV (2) (Geneva, ILO, 1975), pp. 30-47.

equipment and services. Their role of defending the workers' interests makes them a vigilant counterweight to the multinational corporations.

The role of the unions in negotiating co-operation contracts was mentioned very pertinently by J. L. Moynot during our Institute's Geneva Symposium on the social implications of a new international economic order. Echoing an idea put forward by Georges Séguy, Secretary-General of the French CGT, he emphasized that "the trade unions should be associated, in an appropriate manner, with the negotiation of the social aspects of co-operation contracts".[19]

If I dwell on the role of the workers, it is for a fundamental reason: the relationship between the development of the world of labour and the emergence of a new international economic order is worth examining. Just as the nineteenth century saw a dawning awareness of the social injustice of the productive relations which had issued from the industrial revolution, so in recent years the world has come to realize the economic inequality between the industrialized countries and the developing countries, those "proletarian nations". Both periods, that is to say, have this point in common: perception of an unequal and unjust relationship between rich and poor. The similarity of circumstances has induced an identical reaction, which has gradually assumed an institutional form; the *coalition* of all those who recognize their inability to remedy the situation in isolation and who therefore wish to get together, so as to make up by numbers for the position of inferiority in which they find themselves. In both cases, the purpose is to create the conditions for conducting a discussion on a basis of equality. Collective negotiation thus becomes the chosen instrument of the movement for a new international economic order.[20]

---

[19] J. L. Moynot added, in clarification, that "This does not mean that we insist on being a contracting party. It means that, in our view, every contract should, in principle, be supplemented by an agreement on the social aspects, negotiated with the trade union organizations. Should the negotiations not result in an agreement with the trade unions concerned, the unions, on the basis of the views put forward during the discussions, would at least have a definite basis on which to act in ensuring respect for the interests of the workers involved."

[20] See J. de Givry: "International Economic Relations and the Lessons of Industrial Relations", *International Labour Review* (Geneva, ILO), Vol. 113, No. 3, May-June 1976.

The importance of the international organizations

The international organizations play a dual role: they provide the world community with a forum in which contradictory views can be expressed and with a work place where solutions to these contradictions can be hammered out. Mr. Kurt Waldheim is fond of reminding his hearers that antagonistic interests need an arena in which they can be voiced and reconciled; otherwise tensions may be aggravated and relative strength may become the only significant relationship among peoples.

The very concept of the new order and the programme and strategies accompanying it have largely emerged from discussions conducted in the various international organizations. As a universal organization, the United Nations should play a more active role in the establishment of a new international order. It should, for example, reinforce its programming and executive mission with a parallel effort to foment action.

—The international organizations' planning and executive function will certainly grow in so far as the world's problems can only be solved at the multilateral level; logically, therefore, the United Nations and its specialized agencies are specifically designed to fulfil this function. The failings in this respect recorded up to now can be remedied, on the one hand, by a better conceptual definition of their functions and, on the other, by providing the means of action that have sometimes been lacking.

—The organizations' "fomenting" function is of a quite different nature. It consists not in the elaboration of operational concepts but in the mobilization of energies.

It is a commonplace to point out that, in enforcing the execution of its decisions, the United Nations lacks the power of sanction possessed by States. But it is, I think, quite wrong to believe, on these grounds, that because it has limited coercive powers, the United Nations is condemned to ineffectiveness or to the provision of "technical assistance". This view would seem to be based on the idea that all United Nations recommendations are rules of law, involving obligations; whereas, quite apart from any danger of incurring sanctions Member States may come to see that the observance and implementation of United Nations directives would be more profitable than to violate or ignore them. This means that the United Nations is capable, by its "fomenting" function, of putting teeth into the movement for the introduction of a new international economic order and its various social implications. In return this would call for an increase in the resources made available to the United Nations for the implementation of its normative and operational programmes.

But for this to happen, it is essential that the United Nations should cease to be seen as the exact reflection of the existing world of domination which forms the very basis for the present demand for a new international order. In the first place, there are those who give the impression of wishing to wield their power by their veto, thus themselves creating the basis for the "politization" they deplore. There are also the press and information media which, only too often, confine themselves to reporting resolutions or declarations of the moment and dramatizing the debates to which they give rise, instead of describing the immense amount of technical work carried out day after day by the specialized agencies. In the public's eye, therefore, the United Nations is reduced to a sounding-box for the use of those who confuse invective with action and who take refuge in diatribes recalling Shakespeare's phrase, "full of sound and fury, signifying nothing".

These reflections may seem particularly apposite at a time when the United States Government, prompted by certain powerful lobbies, seems bent on calling into question the operation of certain agencies which have a universal scope. Its decision to withdraw from the International Labour Organisation which, according to certain Washington experts, is becoming increasingly politicized, jeopardizes, in the words of Edmond Maire of the French CFDT, "the possibility of holding a genuine dialogue within the international organizations". That decision calls, therefore, for certain comments.

The tribulations of the ILO or pluralism in question

Mr. Al Khatabi, Moroccan Minister, one of those who, with outstanding competence, has served as Chairman of the ILO's Governing

Body, once commented on the ILO, its structure and its current
preoccupations, in a way which clearly reflects the general attitude
of the developing countries towards this institution:

> "More and more, we in the third world are being reduced to
> a single possibility: that of speaking about our problems in all
> the international fora. To deprive us of this possibility is to
> constrict yet further the channels of dialogue and participation.
> And since we should steer clear of all fanaticism, whether of the
> right or of the left, nothing that may arouse fanaticism should
> be invoked at the meeting-place of nations."

Personally, I take the view that all international institutions are
political by nature; even if they concentrate on the technical aspects
of human development, they are immersed in a political environment
which gives them form and substance. This is particularly true of the
International Labour Organisation whose terms of reference relate to
all aspects of workers' living conditions and environment in all parts
of the world and which, with its tripartite structure, seems to me the
international agency which best conforms to the spirit of the Preamble
of the United Nations Charter: "We, the peoples of the United
Nations . . . ".

An eminent American, David A. Morse, who for over 20 years was
Director-General of the ILO, devoted a lot of honest thought to this
question. His conclusions are in line with my present thesis:

> "I think politics will always be with us in the ILO", he said at
> the International Labour Conference in 1956. "It is time", he
> went on, "that we cast aside any remaining illusions that this
> could ever be a purely technical body. We deal here in the ILO
> in human values. Our discussions and decisions reflect what
> people want their world to be like. This is not everywhere the
> same. Different people place the highest value on different
> things—and here I am not speaking alone of material things but
> of social, moral and spiritual things. People strive to attain their
> objectives in social and political movements which sometimes
> come into collision and into conflict. This may be stating the

obvious but it is the point from which, it seems to me, all international action starts."[21]

Mr. Morse returned to the subject at the 1957 Conference and said:

"We cannot impose one man's or one nation's conception of freedom upon the whole world. We cannot deny the lessons which any single people have learned from their history, even though they seem to differ from our own experience. To try to impose freedom in this way would destroy the very nature of freedom itself. It would offend what I call the dignity and self-respect of a people. . . . We cannot assume that the objectives for which this organisation was established are universally accepted or that where they are accepted people mean the same things by them."

Obviously, Mr. Morse had failed to convince his own compatriots and we are back in the times of Foster Dulles: "I want everything, in full and all at once, otherwise I refuse."

At a time when President Carter has found in himself and in his people the resources necessary to propose a just solution of the very complex and difficult problem of Panama which is satisfactory to the people primarily concerned, it is to be hoped that, in the United Nations and the ILO, the facts of a pluralistic world will be recognized by everybody and that the spirit of negotiation and solidarity will prevail, even if, for a while, the United States Government takes its time to look at the question more carefully with a view to more appropriate action in the future. The whole world is interested in the question of work—its nature, its organization, its purpose—and that is why it was already included in the Treaty of Versailles.[22] Who

---

[21] Opening the 63rd session of the International Labour Conference in June 1977, Dr. Haase, representing the Government of the Federal Republic of Germany and speaking as the Chairman of the Governing Body of the ILO, reverted to the subject and said, with utmost clarity: "Our organization is not a non-political institution. It cannot be so, because it is concerned with the social problems of the world and your decisions and actions in this regard constitute social policy." ILO, 63rd Session, Geneva 1977, *Provisional Record No. 5*, p. 3.

[22] Cf. Part XIII of the Treaty of Versailles which, though it was not ratified by the United States Congress, was none the less recognized by the United States Government, which signed it.

can pretend, therefore, that these questions are no longer of concern to the American people? [23]

From the standpoint of universality, the withdrawal of the United States constitutes a grave and even tragic crisis which demands that the ILO should reshape and reorganize itself so that, at long last, a solidarity contract can be negotiated within it which will enable it to make its presence felt in the world of today. [24] The ILO is perfectly capable of surviving in the epoch of "poverty in power" and of providing what appears to be a much-needed example.

"Imagination in power", "creative utopia" are not just slogans: they are also instruments of action capable of mobilizing the workers of the world, the true entrepreneurs, those who make things happen. If the ILO could rise to this level, as Albert Thomas, its true founder, always hoped it would, and if, as some would like it to, it could succeed in ridding itself of all those "tedious, if not pettifogging, aspects which condemn it to a marginal status", then without doubt— paradoxically but surely—the United States would rejoin and play a leading part in its activities. And not only the United States, but other countries, including China, which has up until now stayed away.

In my view there is no doubt at all that if the nations were really mobilized in order to create a new international order, with the ILO taking a bold and active part aimed primarily at the essential concerns of the young people of today, the United States would quickly negotiate some formula for making its presence felt and for keeping an eye on

[23] I am not at all certain that, in the world of international institutions, the Americans will find an organization whose structure and operations meet their wishes and demands as fully as do those of the ILO. To keep on insisting not only that nothing in the structure be changed but also that the ways in which the problems of concern to a deeply frustrated majority are expressed be strictly controlled, means running the risk of undermining, if not destroying, not only one's own advantages, but values that are essential to all. In this connection it is interesting to read J. J. Oechslin: "La crise du tripartisme à l'Organisation internationale du Travail", in *Droit social* (Paris), No. 12, December 1977.

[24] It remains true, as Mr. Francis Blanchard, Director-General of the ILO, has said, that "the ILO, like every human institution, can be improved, but for 60 years it has given more tangible proofs of its usefulness and of its vitality than of its failings". It should not be forgotten that, in 1969, the ILO was awarded the Nobel Peace Prize and that, in the eyes of many, its *technical* work remains unequalled.

developments. The American people—like all the other peoples, of Bavaria or Arabia, Soweto, Amazonia or Uzbekistan—cannot allow a whole world, the world of work, to take shape and develop without them, apart from them and, above all, against them.

But here I must utter a word of warning: it is a mistake to try to confuse the categories. Since the dispute we are talking about seems to have originated in the adoption of certain political attitudes, it seems reasonable to suggest that any resolution or declaration corresponding to such attitudes must be based on the Constitution of the organization concerned and on the rules laid down by that organization in its particular field of competence. This doesn't seem to be asking too much of human intelligence. Politics—yes, that's inevitable; but *qualified* politics, free from abuse, and expressed in decent terms. George Meany would then doubtless find it opportune to reflect again on the questions that worry him.

What is important today is forward-looking concerted action by the social partners leading to the emergence of a new structure which will facilitate the renewal needed to promote the rights of man, as reaffirmed *collectively.*

In the meantime, one field in which it seems that action can be taken without delay is that of international intervention in major development projects. We must get away from the sort of administrative bureaucracy that thinks in terms of man/months or diminutive "country programming" which involved the granting of five fellowships here and there or the extension for one year of the mission of a second-rate expert to a minister perpetually in search of advice.

Many people hope that the international organizations will move firmly in the direction of mobilizing resources for vigorous action on a number of broad fronts of vital importance, within a viable regional framework and on the basis of projects common to a number of countries.

Parallel to this form of international co-operation and apart from the emergency assistance provided in case of need, the contractual solidarity we advocate should make it possible to give support to local projects aimed, in the first place, at meeting the needs of "the humble, the obscure and the common soldiers: those whose basic needs include not only food and housing, but also work, health, education, and a little peace and freedom.[25]

This means taking seriously, before it is too late, the views of the International Labour Organisation which, in 1976, made the problems of meeting basic needs and of employment the subject of its World Conference. What is the use, indeed, of industrial and technological development if the peoples have great difficulty in claiming even their right to live? Today, what the peoples need is to be freed from destitution, to have a guaranteed livelihood, to enjoy good health, to have an honourable job, to participate more actively in the affairs of their country, to have no need to fear oppression or insecurity, and to receive a proper education. These are the aspirations of the "underdeveloped"—"Untermenschen", as they have been called—who at present are "condemned", in Paul-Marc Henry's phrase, "to live in conditions which render these legitimate desires illusory".[26] The essential objective of any solidarity contract is to help towards the satisfaction of these desires, not by day-to-day improvisations, but by long-term remedies which will be lasting because they are selected and implemented with a view to the survival of mankind as a whole.

The elimination of murder and violence

In previous chapters, I have several times referred to armaments expenditures and their impact on resources for development. This entitles me, perhaps, to put forward a proposal that I have already mentioned at certain meetings of the Club of Rome to which I was invited.

I suggest that certain modestly endowed countries—like Costa Rica—should decide to do without national armed forces and to confine their defence measures to the police needed in any society.

[25]I stress these essential values, these absolute and non-quantifiable needs that John Stuart Mill had in mind when he wrote: "It is better to be a human being dissatisfied than a pig satisfied; better to be Socrates dissatisfied than a fool satisfied. And if the fool, or the pig, is of a different opinion, it is because they know only one side of the question."

[26] P.-M. Henry: Statement to the Round Table on the occasion of the 10th Anniversary of the Encyclical "Populorum Progressio", IILS, Geneva, 24 March 1977. Published in *Progrès des peuples et solidarité mondiale* (Geneva, IILS, 1977), pp. 29-41.

I suggest that these countries should inform the international community[27] of their decision and ask it to protect them in the event of aggression resulting from frontier disputes or for any other reason. I am convinced that this would constitute the basis of a solidarity contract and would help promote the genuine development of the countries concerned.

Certainly, detailed studies will be required before such ideas find widespread support and can become a reality. But what seems to me still more urgent is that *credible* countries, capable of setting a real *force of example*, should launch political initiatives in this field.

This idea, put forward at meetings in Madrid and Algiers of the Club of Rome has made but little headway so far, but I still hope that it will soon be given priority. For this reason, I should like to draw attention to the views of Inga Thorson, the Swedish specialist in disarmament problems, which are on the same lines as my proposals. Her analyses throw doubt on the traditional theory of power, based precisely on those armed forces whose disappearance we have the right to demand so as to avoid the conflicts which kill without settling anything. Moreover, once a country's budget is relieved of military expenditure, there will be an opportunity for tax reductions and social investments for the benefit of the majority of the people. And, further, in the context of the "anti-system" we wish to create, this will also make possible a reduction in police forces, since fewer offensive weapons are in circulation.

---

[27]I speak of the international community and not merely of the United Nations, the Security Council or the Disarmament Committee, etc., because I wish to include in the term international public *opinion* and to endow it with strength and responsibility, *vis-à-vis* the various pressure groups organized by particular interests. I would like also, along with millions of other men, to manifest my belief in the last message of Raoul Follereau:
> "There is only one alternative left to the world: we must love each other or vanish
> We must choose—at once, and for ever.
> Yesterday the knell, tomorrow hell.
> The apocalypse is just around the corner.
> Young men and young girls, the world over,
> *You* are the ones who will say *no* to the
> suicide of the human race . . ."

Cf. "J'institue pour légataire universelle la jeunesse du monde" (I make the youth of the world my universal heir) (Testament of R. Follereau, December 1977).

In his book, *Things to Come*, Herman Kahn—despite the fact that he has been described as the "futurologist of power"—adds another argument which is not to be ignored. He writes: "War and the use of armed forces across national frontiers in general, will increasingly be regarded as abnormal and unusable, yet it will always be there. . . . More significant, plausible situations in which force would be relevant or useful have become very difficult to imagine." [28] And here I raise the following impertinent question: If today we really had to face a universal conflagration in which all the currently available forces of destruction were engaged, what would be the use of the "little" armies of the "little" countries of the "feeble" Third or Fourth World? The answer is: none at all. No use at all for the peoples concerned and no long commentaries are needed to justify this assertion. This being the case—an innocent truth, but a truth nevertheless—would it not be better to invest all our resources in the urgent war of common development, *a war which we can win if we all pull together*? That is the option for which I seek support. I call it the "Solidarity Contract".

At this point it does not seem misplaced to refer to another evil that today is destroying certain industrial societies from within: violence, terrorism and the taking of hostages.

The Baader-Meinhof Group's reputation in this respect is already made. The drama which, in October 1977, reached its climax in Mogadiscio, through an example of worldwide co-operation unprecedented in the history of skyjacking, suggests that a solidarity contract is necessary for the reshaping and the survival of all our societies.

But here, as in the case of drugs, to which I shall refer later, a real solidarity contract, instead of treating the disease only in its final stage—that of repression—should propose a choice of essence and existence to all the young people whose revolt is not always aimed at money, a career or honours, but often demands a different kind of society. As Helmut Schmidt himself said on the morrow of the Mogadiscio operation, "Many young people disapprove the exaggerated stress put by some on the enjoyment of material goods, thus relegating to the background the sense of the meaning of life."

[28] H. Kahn and B. Bruce-Briggs: *Things to Come* (New York, Macmillan, 1972), pp. 122-3.

This identification of the problem before us confirms two lines of thought and action.

The first consists in examining all the possibilities of internationalizing dissuasive action, as I have just recommended in proposing international solidarity to back up the peoples which have the strength to opt for general disarmament.

For, apart from quite exceptional cases, is it really possible for every government to maintain on a permanent basis a *corps d'élite* such as that which carried out the Mogadiscio operation? And even if this were possible would it not involve the risk of building up the police systems of States whose structures are already contested beyond the point at which control is possible, so that they would constitute a supreme peril for democracy itself?

Secondly, I should like to repeat that the remedy for the violence of despair, frustration and short-sightedness requires a *utopia*, and I see this in the society of poverty and hence of justice, in development based on solidarity, a "Co-operative Republic" allowing more scope for the expression of other than material values.[29] To eliminate murder and violence is to protect life, the primary basis of any real solidarity contract: "Thou shalt not kill." But to live is not merely to exist, it is also to have the means of developing one's participation in mankind as a whole. I come back, therefore, to one of those basic needs, the satisfaction of which calls for negotiated solidarity: food.

Food co-operation going beyond aid

In the field of food co-operation, the solidarity contract would not simply confine itself to an aid programme for the benefit of needy countries or social groups.

Apart from the short-term satisfaction of food needs, such a contract

[29] An idea expressed by Dr. Philip Potter, General Secretary of the World Council of Churches, Geneva, is particularly worth mentioning: "The person who is in thrall to a system, whether intellectual, moral, economic, social or ideological, becomes intolerant towards all who question it. Such a system is violent in itself, for it violates human rights. It calls forth counter-violence and is the foundation for the escalation of violence . . . I feel that the structural intolerance of our societies is the foundation for the growing violence we see today throughout the world." (Statement to the 11th World Day of Peace, Geneva, 11 January 1978).

would also identify the ways and means of developing local agricultural resources. Thus a plan would be drawn up for a specified period, providing for the gradual reduction of food aid in inverse proportion to the progress made, through the development of agriculture, towards a self-sufficient economy.[30]

In these conditions, the recipient State cannot limit its role to that of a distributor. It becomes an active partner by undertaking a programme for the expansion and rationalization of food growing, supported by the active participation of the rural workers in the areas suffering from a food deficiency.

The terms of the contract, as well as the evaluation and control procedures during implementation, should provide a guarantee that the foodstuffs supplied and the agricultural co-operation undertaken would be of real benefit to the populations concerned.

This guarantee of effectiveness should provide a first incentive to the industrialized countries to develop this new type of food co-operation. But, in addition to a demonstration of their generosity, they would find in this policy a way of redirecting their growth by developing agricultural technology and production in the sectors in which the needs of the Third World are at present most acute, and even of changing its nature by adopting a new style of consumption in the rich countries, avoiding waste and excessive food consumption.

Reciprocally, solidarity practised in this way opens up new avenues of development for the countries and regions suffering from malnutrition. From the moment the contract was signed, the peasant and wage-earning masses most seriously affected would be assured of escaping the tragedy threatening them. At the same time, through their own organization, and with appropriate technical support, they would take part in a process of making the most of the earth's resources, aimed at the satisfaction of their needs.

The solidarity contract would be—as it is designed to be—at the centre of a self-reliant and self-maintained development process.

---

[30] For a critical analysis of the various forms of food aid and their incorporation into the development policies of the beneficiary countries, see: *L'aide alimentaire: de la redistribution des produits au financement des investissements*, Th. Pang, Cahiers de l'Institut des Sciences économiques et sociales, N. 34 (Fribourg, Editions Universitaires, 1974).

In this particular context, it would take the form of:

—the activization of local economic and social life: the management and distribution of aid, and the organization of production by the peasants, farmers and craftsmen;

—promoting education in the rural community, which would thus become aware of its role in the proposed development strategy, in particular, that the community itself determines the needs to be met and the consequent production priorities.

The roots of a "terrifying" evil

Still more concretely, I should like to link this type of solidarity contract with the solution of a social problem which depends more than is generally believed on the organization of the rural world in the developing countries. I am referring to drug addiction, the evil that is engrossing the attention of all governments and all socially responsible people, particularly in the industrialized countries.

No country, in fact, is spared by this modern form of human enslavement. It is a worldwide phenomenon, the suppression of which inevitably calls for general action in concert, co-operation and solidarity.

The international community has already adopted a certain number of measures which have resulted in the 1961 "Single Convention on Narcotic Drugs", supplemented by a Protocol in 1972. Following this lead, we may try to imagine effective strategies aimed at destroying the infernal circuit whose various stages are: the illicit production of drugs, their marketing and their consumption.

The phenomenon of drug addiction lays bare the psychological and personal tragedy of individuals who, through the use of drugs, sometimes have little left of their humanity beyond their membership of the human race. The tragedy has also a social dimension because the victims, cast out of society, go to swell the ranks of the desperate, while awaiting the fatal outcome.

Dr. Olievenstein, who is conducting an interesting experiment in France, says that, in 1976, more than 40 boys and girls died from taking drugs;[31] it is a measure of the extent of the evil that, in 1977,

---

[31] In Geneva, a non-governmental group, the "Permanence des jeunes", gives the following figures of deaths in France due to the ingestion of drugs: 1 in 1969; 11 in 1971; 6 in 1972; 29 in 1974; 37 in 1975; and 54 in 1976.

among the 150 addicts—including 80 per cent of heroin addicts—who attempted a cure the majority returned to their habitual sphere.

In this field, the degradation of some has its corollary in the criminality of others—traffickers, chemists, "salesmen of death"— tempted by the lure of gain from a lucrative and criminal trade.

In most cases, acts relating to the sale and use of narcotic drugs are legally punishable, with greater or lesser severity depending on the effectiveness of the police and legal system of the country in which this type of delinquency occurs.

The current tendency to attempt to rehabilitate addicts by appropriate forms of treatment while intensifying the fight against the illicit drug traffic should certainly be encouraged.

But to eradicate the evil, it is essential—despite the failure of previous attempts—to make still more energetic efforts to control production and sometimes even to go further and destroy certain of the raw materials from which dangerous drugs are manufactured.

It will then be easier, at the other end of the "connection", to discourage the purchase of a product which is gradually disappearing from the market. This would promote the "demarketing" of drugs— to apply the concept which I introduced above—so that the circuits serving the international traffic can be dismantled from their point of departure.

The phenomenon of drug addiction originates, in fact, in specific agricultural activities: the growing of the opium poppy, of cannabis or of the coca leaf. For the growers, whether Burmese, Turks or Mexicans, these crops have for generations constituted their principal means of livelihood. They owe their development to the weight of tradition, to the need for an income to live on, or again to outside pressures. As there is usually no intention to do harm, the growers find it difficult to see the unlawfulness of their activity. How, therefore, can they be expected to give up an economic activity which they regard as perfectly normal, merely because of the dangers resulting from the marketing and consumption of their product?

Opium growing for the producer, like the consumer's craving for the drug, is a social problem. Governments at either end of the "connection" feel the need and the urgency of immediate intervention. But the effects will be slight if the action taken remains at the national level.

This is particularly true of the countries in which the crops are grown. These countries, which often lack the means of controlling the economy, find difficulty in taking the decision which is called for here: replacement of the type of farming that supplies the narcotics trade. In view of their meagre resources and the economic consequences of abolishing the traditional activities, the producing countries cannot alone bear the costs of the operation. It is essential, therefore, to launch a concerted action of the producing and consuming countries, what I would call a solidarity contract, the purpose of which would be to eliminate the dangerous crops and replace them by forms of farming at least as profitable from the economic standpoint and unquestionably better from the social standpoint.

In addition to attacking the evil at its roots, the negotiators of such a contract would be laying the foundations of a new rural development policy in the areas in question, if they extended the operation to include measures for the education and training of the peasant masses.

It is hard to imagine that, faced by the threat to youth and by the rapid growth in the use of drugs which is sapping the foundations of many societies, the United Nations Member States, whatever their ideological system, will prove incapable of finding the political will necessary for the conclusion of such a contract.

The grave problem referred to above illustrates the urgent necessity for co-development: the interdependence of peoples and their joint responsibility in view of the inability of individual countries to act alone.

The example of a solidarity contract for the gradual elimination of the sources of the supply of drugs may appear to be confined to the pathological aspects of world relations. But the subject is not without importance, because it is a matter of universally recognized urgency.

Other types of contracts may be mentioned: joint research to overcome cancer, contracts for cultural exchanges freed from any form of cultural hegemony,[32] contracts relating to worker migration

[32] An idea of Joseph Ki-Zerbo's is worth mentioning: "Every economic programme launched by the industrialized countries for the benefit of the under-equipped countries should obligatorily comprise a culture section which would constitute the real meaning of the project for its beneficiaries. Can one imagine a cultural Lomé Convention? but it would be quite as essential as the other." (*Culture et développement*, Geneva, IILS, November 1976).

and to the living conditions, training and health of migrant workers and their repatriation to their country of origin.[33]

Another example: the twenty-third session of the United Nations General Assembly declared the open sea to be "the common heritage of mankind", a concept related to the doctrine that property is held in trust for the benefit of all. The seas and their wealth offer new prospects for human initiative, constituting a major source of technological innovations.

Thus, despite the uncertainties of the Conference on the Law of the Sea, where sovereign egoisms are already obstructing an agreement on concerted action, it remains true that the exploitation of the seabed may offer a field of application for the concept of a solidarity contract.

The North-South dialogue: the need to avoid false issues

Solidarity contracts should not be substitutes or palliatives for the necessary restructuring of international relationships. They imply or call for the implementation of new legally sanctioned economic relations.

Thus, an element of hope—the North-South dialogue—has appeared in the confrontation caused by the recent price-of-energy crisis. The idea was not only brilliant and generous, but completely realistic, and the welcome it received gave grounds for believing that everyone was convinced of the need for such negotiations. But we know now how disappointed were the partners on either side at the end of the exercise.

It seems necessary, therefore, to point out that success would not have been so far off if certain factors had been taken into account:

---

[33] In Switzerland, an important initiative significantly entitled *"Etre solidaires"* received 50,000 signatures. It protested against the humiliating status of seasonal workers, whose conditions of work and of family life are very far from the international standards for foreign workers.

We hope that a referendum in this sense will rehabilitate Switzerland in the eyes of the world, painfully surprised by the initiative of James Schwarzenbach.

The French *Conseil d'Etat* has fortunately put a check on measures designed to limit the arrival in France of the families of immigrant workers. But has the danger really been removed? Has Lionel Stoleru—under the guise of promoting "full employment in a period of slow growth"—said his last word?

In the first place, it is undesirable to try to work outside the framework of the United Nations in which the small countries feel that their aspirations can be freely expressed and in which *collective* negotiation enables them to take part in determining the objectives which concern them.

Many countries had the impression that the North-South dialogue was a sort of unwarranted substitution for the regular organs of international consensus which finds expression in the United Nations. Thus Mr. Pérez Guerrero,[34] one of the co-presidents of the Paris Conference, thought it necessary to state on a number of occasions that: "The North-South dialogue in which a significant, but nevertheless limited, number of countries (27 participants, one of which counts as 9) are engaged, must either succeed or must hand over to the United Nations . . . As far as any follow-up machinery is concerned, we think that it should also come within the framework of the Organization that comprises the whole of the international community, with very few exceptions. The appropriate instance may be supplemented by other bodies—such as the Brandt Commission, originally promoted by Mr. McNamara—*but what we cannot accept is an attempt by a small number of governments, or of a 'Committee of Wise Men' however wise they may be, to interfere directly in our dialogue.*"

Such an attitude may seem surprising, but its importance cannot be questioned, especially at a time when serious doubts are being expressed here and there concerning the effectiveness of the United Nations and of the majority votes recorded there. Those who ridicule the "automatic majority" or who express concern at the operation of the Organization seem to lose sight of the fact that the majority reflects a reality: a majority of the world's population and thus of its human resources, a majority of natural resources, and also a majority of problems, sufferings and misfortunes, often originating from

[34] See, in particular, the Report of the Round Table on the 10th Anniversary of the Encyclical "Populorum Progressio", IILS, Geneva, 24 March 1977, published in *Progrès des peuples et solidarité mondiale* (Geneva, IILS, 1977), p. 50. See also on the North-South dialogue the excellent article by Hernán Santa Cruz in *Transition*, Bulletin of the Centre international pour le développement, Paris, July 1977.

outside.[35] This majority may sometimes express itself anarchically and in its own way. But is it to be silenced by force or by any other means? Let us beware! "The fatal disease of the body politic", warned Robespierre, "is not anarchy; it is tyranny."

Another factor that might lead to the success of the North-South dialogue is to speak the language of an intelligent social prospective. It is, in fact, regrettable that the Paris Conference concentrated primarily on the present, using outmoded analytical models. For example, much energy was expended on talking about the price of raw materials, the international division of labour, trade and aid. These are important factors, but to couch the dialogue in these terms is to continue the language of the colonial era, with the pattern of bargaining being modified only by the new balance of forces.

When the "spice route" turns into a dangerous dead-end

Of course, slogans and exclamations are not enough to soften or modify the rules of an exchange market designed for the benefit of the strongest and most violent party.

The small producers, seeking a livelihood from their cotton or ground-nuts, are demanding that their situation be made tolerable without further delay. We cannot turn them off with talk of possible future reforms of structure. That is why every move designed to put an end to the deterioration of terms of trade and monetary erosion, from which the poorest suffer most, fits into the framework for setting up a new international order. Thus, some specialists consider that the Lomé Convention, which came into force in 1976, constituted an improvement over the previously prevailing situation in the commercial, industrial, technical and financial fields. The increase in the number of adherents (on the one hand, the nine countries of the Common

---

[35] In a recent work, *Un métier unique au monde* (Paris, Stock, 1977), Kurt Waldheim, Secretary-General of the United Nations, recognizes this fact and explains it as follows: "The newly liberated countries which now constitute the majority of the international community, claim the place to which they are entitled and expect to receive equal treatment. They are increasingly impatient of Western centricity which is the source, in their eyes, of misunderstanding and prejudice."

Market, and, on the other, 46 countries in Africa, the Carribbean and the Pacific area (ACP)) makes it possible to envisage a less "colonial" type of relationship. What is more, the Lomé Convention introduced a new mechanism—the stabex—to help stabilize income derived from certain types of export, although not affecting the actual market prices. Thus, for any specific group of products, if the income from exports to Common Market countries falls below a certain pre-determined level, the loss is compensated for by a financial transfer to the associated country concerned. As Claude Cheysson has often pointed out, this effort to stabilize resources in foreign currency can enable the countries concerned to avoid the consequences of serious lack of foresight in development planning. But it gives rise to some very serious questions. First and foremost, and primarily in consideration of the strategic interest of mineral products for the industrial growth of the Common Market countries, we are obliged to note that out of the twelve groups of products covered by the stabex mechanism there is only one mineral, namely iron. Yet, for several of the countries concerned, other mineral products represent a significant part of their exports. We need only to mention, for example, the copper of Zaïre and Zambia, both of which are associated with the EEC.

Another equally important question: there exist clauses restricting the transfer of funds in cases where one of the ACP countries might decide to change its export policy. Such clauses limit considerably the possibilities of developing a structural production policy which might consist, for example, in organizing the market supply of a product in agreement with the other producers, or, on a national scale, replacing export crops with food crops in some areas.

And finally, it must not be forgotten that, except in extreme cases of force majeure, a reimbursement procedure is provided for. Thus, the exporting countries run the risk of not being able to take full advantage of market prices in so far as they have, in most cases, previously benefited from a financial transfer.

For all these—and many other—reasons, the developing countries as a whole, in the framework of what is commonly called the "Group of 77", have been led to promote and support an "Integrated Programme for Commodities". This is a proposal of fundamental importance for the application of a new international order to questions

of trade and development. It was first put forward in the action programme adopted by the United Nations General Assembly at its Sixth
Special Session on 1 May 1974. Two years later, in 1976, in Nairobi,
at the Fourth United Nations Conference on Trade and Development,
a resolution was adopted, based on the report of Gamani Corea, the
Secretary-General, which defined the objectives and outlined the
practical measures envisaged in the integrated programme.

The latter applies to ''a comprehensive range of commodities of export
interest to developing countries''. The idea is to set in motion a series
of simultaneous negotiations, concerning the main primary products,[36]
involving, for each of them: the setting up of buffer stocks, arrangements
regarding prices, and long-term multilateral agreements between producers and importers. Over and above these agreements relating to
specific products, the integrated programme would include a *common
fund for the complementary financing of the various stocks, a mechanism for stabilizing the income from exports and commercial measures
designed to improve the access of primary and semi-finished products
originating in developing countries, to the markets of the industrialized
countries.*

The importance of the integrated programme lies in three of its main
characteristics. In the first place, it does not confine itself, as does
the stabex, to an *ex post facto* correction of the fluctuations in market
prices but, rather, includes measures relating to the level of production
with a view to reaching its specific goal—to improve income from
exports. Secondly, it places stress on other objectives which are also
of basic importance to the Third World, such as encouraging food
production and the processing of primary products in the country
where they are produced. And finally, the programme highlights the
reciprocal nature of the benefits it would bring: for the importing
countries, a certainty of steady market supply and the elimination of
periodical ''price flare-ups'', and for the producing countries, a guarantee of external resources and better planning of the various sectors
of production. Thus, in this case we could invoke the notion of the
solidarity contract, since the integrated programme requires mutual

---

[36] At present, the list includes 18 products: *vegetable and animal products:* bananas,
tropical woods, cocoa, coffee, rubber, cotton, hard fibres, vegetable oils, jute, sugar,
tea, meat; *mineral products*: bauxite, copper, tin, iron, manganese, phosphates.

agreements on a series of long-term objectives.

Some questions arise, however, with regard to the conditions and the forms in which it may be implemented. In the first place, the role of the market in such agreements would have to be clearly defined. Would the purpose be to restrict it—by a policy of quotas and multilateral agreements—or only to correct its effects—by stabilizing prices and export income? This leads to a second question: how can the integrated programme incite the Third World countries to reconvert to production for the home market, limiting and controlling their foreign trade as a result? In the third place, because of its comprehensive nature, the implementation of the programme requires that the agreements be respected: this means the strict application of export quotas, supply agreements, etc. Any failure to respect the agreements would bring us back to the present state of chaos. Only the political will of the parties—the basis of the solidarity contract—can enable us to avoid such deterioration.

The negotiations undertaken in the framework of the "integrated programme" are, in fact, proving laborious, while at the same time there have been serious delays in the application of previously concluded agreements. Thus, of the 18 products concerned, agreement has been reached in respect of five, discussions are underway with regard to three or four others, and as far as the rest are concerned, no negotiations have started.

If the delays and lengthy procedures that have proved necessary in order to negotiate and sign some of the agreements concerning certain products became the general rule—and this would undoubtedly suit some people—it would take us *more than a century* to succeed in carrying out the present programme!

I need hardly say that the developing countries refuse to submit to the rule of such exploitative manoeuvres, which are contrary to common sense. They want to move ahead much faster and will not stand for having their export income, which is already weak and irregular, completely ravaged by the erosion of currency, compound interest payments, and the ever increasing burden of foreign debts.[37]

37 The recent initiative of a few countries (Canada, The Netherlands, Sweden) with a view to promoting an international policy of cancelling the debts of Third World countries has not been widely followed. Those countries who could have a decisive impact on the solution of one of the most painful problems of our time would certainly not agree to such a policy.

For a Solidarity Contract

There is one question of the utmost priority which must be raised—
no trace of which is discernible in any programme or schedule for
negotiations that I know of, either in the UNCTAD or the North-South
dialogue. That is, the role of stock markets—of New York, London
or Paris—which have a decisive influence on everything relating to raw
materials prices. According to those who have studied the question most,
if we wish to increase the value of the Third World exports we must
take some decisions at this level that will require a great deal of courage
since they will attack certain strongholds sheltering certain secret and
privileged agencies which, acting through various obscure persons, make
it possible for unidentifiable centres of decision to exercise a baleful
influence on the lives of millions of people. The time has come for
these strongholds to be brought out into the full light of day, not only
to satisfy the curiosity of the mind but to enable us to take the necessary
action for our deliverance.

As the Senegalese Makhtar Diouf so rightly said of the stock market,
"That is where the prices of raw materials are determined, from day
to day. That is where the lot of the producers of developing countries is
decided, without their even being represented there . . . Prices for manufactured goods are fixed unilaterally by the undertakings which produce
and market them. Why shouldn't it be the same for the primary
products?"[38]

The important role of the stock markets and, hence, of the business
world, leads us to wonder why their "partners" of the Third World
are so unaccountably absent. Take, for example, the influence
exercised by the Union des Industries de la Communauté Economique
Européenne (UNICE) within the Common Market, particularly in all
matters concerning relations with the associated countries. Faced
with such a powerful employers' organization—of which the Anglo-
Dutch group UNILEVER is a member, for example—how can we
explain that the governments of the ACP countries are reluctant to
encourage their workers' organizations, members of co-operatives
and all other producers, to make a vigorous collective effort to
participate as directly as possible in the negotiations which are of
primary concern to them?

[38] Cf. M. Diouf: *Echange inégal et ordre économique international* (Dakar, Nouvelles
Editions Africaines, 1977).

In fact, the compensatory measures provided for by stabex and other formulae are designed to rectify the effect of decisions taken by the stock markets. Logically, what is needed is to question these decisions themselves. Thus theoretical research and political action should be directed on a priority basis towards the machinery for fixing raw materials prices. What is needed is for the producers themselves to take this machinery in hand and to integrate into it the real value of their work.[39] Unfortunately, there is at present no such prospect . . .

The continued fragility of the position of the Third World is thus evident, in spite of certain very lucid analyses and undeniably courageous statements. All that we need, in addition, is a strong political will to counter the intransigent and calculated apathy of the powerful as well as the force of inertia which, in practice, hinders the advent of a new international order.

We are also bound to note that the results of a recent Conference on a Common Fund for the financing of international commodity buffer stocks and other measures (November-December 1977) do not in any way give grounds for optimism since the Group of 77

---

[39] The President of the Republic of Senegal, Léopold Sédar Senghor, made some pertinent comments on this subject speaking before the International Labour Conference on 19 June 1971. This Chief of State expressed the wish for the ILO to participate in efforts undertaken to solve the problems raised by the fixing of raw materials prices, with a view to including the *work value* as a recognized component.

Since then, the delegates from a wide range of countries—Romania, Sri Lanka, Mexico—have intervened in support of the Senegalese proposal. It is becoming urgent for the ILO to take up this suggestion, now that efforts are being made to revive the North-South dialogue and particularly in view of the fact that a special session of the General Assembly of the United Nations has been scheduled for 1980 in order to consider the various policies put forward with a view to setting up a new international order.

The urgency of the matter and the need for effective action demand that, prior to, or parallel with, the discussions in the regular organs of the ILO, research institutes, such as the IILS, and independent scientific associations, like the AMPS, should without delay study this question of the fixing of prices on the raw materials market. On this specific subject, reference may be made to the article by Patrick Robineau: "Guidelines for Research with a View to Another Kind of Development" in *Labour and Society* (Geneva, IILS), Vol. 3, No. 2, April 1978.

found itself obliged to ask for a suspension of the discussions.[40]

The Common Fund, which had been accepted in principle both at the close of the Nairobi Conference and at the North-South dialogue in Paris, has been compromised by the hesitations and dilatory arguments of certain countries. Yet everyone knows that it constitutes an essential element not only for the stabilization of prices but also for co-ordinating policies and practical measures related to every aspect of the production and marketing of raw materials. As Prebisch wanted, some time ago, the purpose is to facilitate, through this fund, the processing on the spot and consequently the increase in value of agricultural and mineral resources, which will enable the Third World to free itself from the alienating trade in primary products which has been forced upon it like a levy and a scourge ever since the "spice route" was discovered—a veritable impasse, enclosing the most disadvantaged peoples in a vicious circle of increasing destitution.

The creative autonomy of peoples

A pertinent article by Alfred Sauvy[41] stresses the fact that the Third World cannot be expected to mark time indefinitely, selling groundnuts cheaply and buying manufactured articles at ever higher prices. The Third World will industrialize so that it too can produce the more sophisticated goods for its own use, going beyond mere subsistence.

And, in this context, it will not agree to confine itself to the final stage (assembly plants, for example). The Third World intends to master the whole production process from the extraction of raw materials, through manufacturing to marketing. For this purpose, it needs, in an initial stage, technological know-how and capital equipment. As Pierre Drouin[42] has rightly pointed out, this offers the industrialized countries a potential new market.

[40] See, in this connection, U.N. document TD/IPC/CF/CONF/4.7/Add. 2, of 12 December 1977, giving the positions of the various parties concerned.

See also the two basic documents concerning the objectives and machinery of the Integrated Programme for Commodities:—Resolution 93 (IV) adopted by the IVth session of UNCTAD, Nairobi, 30 May 1976. Report of the Secretary-General of UNCTAD, TD/B/C-1/166, of 9 December 1974.

[41] *L'Expansion,* July 1977.   [42] *Le Monde,* 22 July 1977.

But this demand cannot be satisfied unless certain essential conditions
—frequently forgotten in "turnkey" contracts—are observed.

First of all, it should be borne in mind that semifinished products
and certain capital goods are justified only if, in the final stage, they
produce articles in sufficient quantities and at prices within the
purchasing power of the most numerous social groups. To illustrate
this point, I shall mention that in India, for example, 40 per cent of
the population have an income of less than $50 per year, which is
the poverty threshold fixed by the Indians themselves.

The employment position is another criterion for the selection and
adaptation of technologies. To continue with India, it is forecast
that between 1974 and 1984, the male labour force will increase from
152 to 196 million. The creation of jobs on such a scale means getting
away from the methods used hitherto, based on the importation of
capital-intensive technologies, the most evident result of which is
to create "little, relatively prosperous, urbanised pockets in an ocean
of misery", as Ward Morehouse and Jan Sigurdson[43] rightly observe.
This coincides with the views of Mr. Francis Blanchard, Director-
General of the ILO, who, speaking before ECOSOC on 12 July
1977, said:

". . . capital will continue to be too scarce for us to be able to
use only capital-intensive techniques to create employment. At
present such techniques assume an investment of $50,000 to
create one job. The ILO's manpower projections suggest that in
the developing countries, which already have some 300 million
unemployed or under-employed, the working population will
have grown by over 800 million before the year 2000."

Finally, the imported technical processes and capital goods should
be capable of being mastered by the indigenous technicians and
workers who are to apply and use them. Experience shows that the
developing countries which have achieved some success in accelerating
their economic progress, within a framework of social justice and the
mastery of the basic needs of the people, have all adopted the same
strategy: a growing capacity to create, acquire, adapt and, above all,
to use technical solutions suited to their geographical situation and

[43] *Technology and Poverty* by Ward Morehouse and Jan Sigurdson, Lund University,
Sweden, 1977, 4 pp. (roneoed).

to their economic and social conditions. Henceforth, *technological autonomy* is one of the prime aspirations of the Third World countries.

In this connection, Morehouse and Sigurdson suggest the following "research hypothesis": *to declare a ten-year moratorium on new transfers of technology to the developing countries and on the export from those countries of non-processed raw materials.*

I call this a "research hypothesis" aimed at protecting the Third World countries from trade in technology and in raw materials so long as they are in a position of inferiority, thus giving them a chance to launch their autonomous process of industrialization through assimilating the experience already gained.

Here again we can imagine a solidarity contract whose driving force and final objective would be industrial self-reliance, on the same pattern as the agricultural co-operation aiming at self-sufficiency in foodstuffs.

Such contracts may seem utopian, but they are in fact indispensable. Many of the misunderstandings and misapprehensions underlying the North-South dialogue arise from the refusal of the rich countries to grasp the radical nature of the new order demanded by the Third World. Beyond the temporary redistributive mechanisms, the Third World seeks to recover its identity and its own capabilities. As I wrote as far back as 1958,[44] the peoples of the Third World say:

1. "We wish to be the agents of our own progress and no longer merely the beneficiaries of the progress made on our territories;

2. We want to progress rapidly, at the tempo of the modern world, and taking account of the distance we have to make up, and not merely at the rhythm dictated by some false prudence;

3. We want to take over the management of our own affairs and not merely participate in it to a greater or lesser extent."

It is disturbing, to say the least, on reading, for example, the remarkable statement by Mahbub ul Haq at Algiers during the discussion of the RIO Project, to note that now, 20 years afterwards, these aspirations are unchanged.

But a real change is still possible, through negotiated solidarity. Unequal exchanges will be replaced by exchanges that are doubly

---

[44] Albert Tévoédjrè: *L'Afrique révoltée* (Paris, Présence africaine, 1958), p. 19.

complementary, guaranteeing greater well-being to *both* parties to the contract: whether countries or social groups.

It is no longer a question of the international division of labour —even if it is called "new" or "greatly improved". It is no longer a question of "enjoying slavery". It is a question of something quite different: *the development of the creative autonomy of peoples within a readjusted international exchange system.*

Armed with our hope . . .

In consenting to place the aspirations of the peoples in a context of negotiation and contract, we are inviting the world community to realize its interdependence.[45] And we do this *in a spirit of universalism and of uncompromising decolonization.* In this way we discover our common wealth and the need to share it as responsible partners aware that their use of the common heritage in a spirit of poverty affords the best chance of survival. This way of experiencing poverty enhances our capacity for reflection and our chances of attaining the true life of the spirit, which cannot be dissociated from general well-being promoted by our common efforts.

But time is short because famine is spreading and our armaments are piling up the bodies of the victims and the air is not always fit to breathe.

Adam Smith tells the story of a tired traveller who said, "This house threatens to fall down; it won't stand up for long, but it's the devil's luck if it collapses tonight. I'll take the risk and sleep the night here . . . ." Our house is threatening to fall down on us and we are taking unreasonable risks.

If it is true as Jean Ziegler says, that "an eschatology informs history", the still unattainable utopia to which we are tending is "the planetary society built on the basis of strict solidarity where active mutual help will replace the profit motive and where the search for the happiness of all will take the place of contemptible class and national interests".

[45] The collection of essays, *Goals for Mankind,* edited by Ervin Laszlo (New York, Dutton, 1976) and in particular the last chapter (World Solidarity Revolution) is worth reading in this connection.

The Solidarity Contract can lead to an essential stage in this process: that in which we rediscover ourselves and take control of our collective destiny. Between the fatalism and nihilism of despair and a blind or complacent optimism we can still take up the constructive challenge of solidarity, defined and implemented in common. It is only solidarity, in the shape of a contract negotiated between us, that will divert us, I believe, from that desperate flight envisaged by Nietzsche "towards the point where, up to now, all the suns have sunk and been extinguished". Against the background of our poverty, it will confirm the richness of our values and of all our hopes.

Post-scriptum

"The child goes away to the
bush.
Altar, accept water and wood,
That the good power depart
not with the blood!
That the evil power
depart! . . ."
Prayer of the Sage Dogon,
sprinkling the altar of his
ancestors with water to bless
his son before each new
departure.
Sakété (Benin),
21 February 1978

"I shall not ask you all to
become saints. (Yet that would
be the answer.) I shall not bid
you 'Love one another'! (Same
comment.) I shall merely say:
Change this system, which
provides so many opportunities
for hatred, for another which
encourages and calls for
solidarity. Now no such change
will occur in the City . . . save
if it has first taken place
within you. If you would alter
the future, alter yourselves."
(Denis de Rougemont in
L'avenir est notre affaire
(The future is up to us).)

In the history of each of us there are places and dates that have
a far greater meaning than others.

This is what I feel deep within me today in this place where I passed
a youth that is not yet forgotten, on this very date when, a student at
Toulouse and an active member of the FEANF (Student's Federation
of French-speaking Black Africa), I was one of the moving spirits of
the "Anticolonialist Day".

This return to my roots, here, today, is thus of symbolic value for me;
it symbolizes *the recovery by each person of his own sovereignty—
finding full expression in a social discipline openly established and
collectively accepted.*

This is the true aim of the essay that is ending here. And yet, this book
Poverty: Wealth of Mankind may well give rise to highly contradictory comments. Some will find it too unrealistic and be unable
to conceal their scepticism. Others may accept the theories propounded

but will want to enquire into the life of the author himself and his understanding of poverty. By giving vent to their comments and questioning they will all be rendering me the greatest service, and I should like to thank them now.

Collective self-criticism, which I called for from persons in various positions of social responsibility, not forgetting the Third World, would make sense only if it first made each of us take stock of his own self. "That the evil power depart!"

If we get together to give birth to a new political will, we shall have made a lasting contribution to that human revolution which will change us and at the same time change our environment. So if you feel concerned by such considerations, in particular by considerations about a solidarity contract, and if you want to help to delve further into them, I should be grateful if you would kindly write to me at the following address:

> International Institute for Labour Studies[1]
> P. O. Box No. 6
> 1211 Geneva 22
> Switzerland.

> "Our blood must catch fire
> Our whole being must catch fire
> If we are to move the bystanders
> If the world is at last to open its eyes
> Not on our dead bodies
> But on the wounds of the survivors . . ."

Kateb Yacine

---

[1] Founded in Geneva by the International Labour Organisation, the International Institute for Labour Studies aims to assist towards a clearer understanding of social problems and labour problems throughout the world by means of discussion, research and education.

Among its various research programmes is the study of the conditions and forms of a new international order integrating the economic and socio-cultural dimensions of development within a single contract based on the human values of justice, responsibility and solidarity.

Appendices

173

APPENDIX I

Unamortized external public debt (withdrawn and not withdrawn)
of developing countries[1] (with low and medium incomes), 1974
(in $ millions and percentages)

	$ millions	Percentages
Low income countries	38,770.2	100.0
From official sources	34,100.0	88.0
Bilateral	25,221.4	65.1
Multilateral	8,878.6	22.9
From private sources	4,670.2	12.0
Suppliers	1,894.0	4.9
Banks	2,322.7	6.0
Various	453.5	1.1
Medium income countries	75,145.0	100.0
From official sources	42,099.8	56.0
Bilateral	25,072.3	33.4
Multilateral	17,027.5	22.6
From private sources	33,045.2	44.0
Suppliers	8,919.3	11.9
Banks	18,806.5	25.0
Various	5,319.4	7.1
Total	113,915.2	100.0
From official sources	76,199.8	66.9
From private sources	37,715.4	33.1

N.B. The above chart only shows debts, from both public and private sources, which are unamortized or guaranteed by the public sector (governments or official bodies) of beneficiary developing countries. The chart does not include unguaranteed loans granted to private concerns or individuals, the figures of which are not shown in the reports published by the World Bank; nevertheless these form a substantial sum of additional debt incurred by the developing countries.

Source: The above chart is based on the *World Debt Tables: External Public Debt of LDC's,* World Bank, Doc. No. EC-167/76, Vol. 1, 31 October 1976, pp. 114-15.

[1] Excluding member countries of OPEC.

APPENDIX II

Distribution of world exports, by groups of countries,
1960, 1970 and 1975 (in $ billions and percentages)

Whereas the dollar value of exports from developing countries other than members of
OPEC rose from $18.9 billion in 1960 to $97.3 billion in 1975, their share of world
exports dropped from 14.8 per cent in 1960 to 12 per cent in 1970 and 11.1 per cent
in 1975.

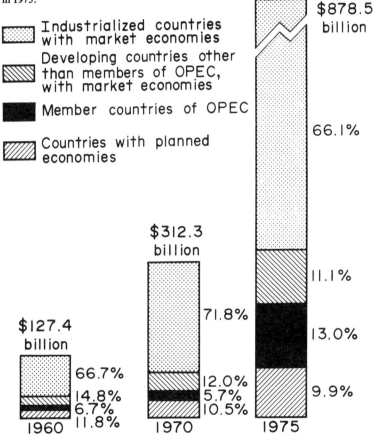

Sources: The figures for 1960 are taken from the *U.N. Monthly Bulletin of Statistics*,
Vol. 19, No. 3, March 1965, special table E; those for 1970 are taken from the *U.N.
Monthly Bulletin of Statistics*, Vol. 30, No. 8, August 1976, special table C; those for
1975 from the *U.N. Monthly Bulletin of Statistics*, Vol. 30, No. 6, June 1976, special
table C.

Appendices

APPENDIX III

Net contribution of official development assistance provided by DAC
(Development Assistance Committee) member countries, 1960 and 1975
(in $ millions, $, and percentages)

Countries listed by order of the amount of their financial contribution[a]	Total contribution ($ millions)		Contribution per inhabitant ($)		Contribution in percentage of GNP	
	1960	1975	1960	1975	1960	1975
Sweden	7	566	.94	69.06	.05	.82
Netherlands	35	604	3.05	44.24	.31	.75
Norway	5	184	1.39	45.92	.11	.66
France	823	2,091	18.07	39.65	1.38	.62
Australia	59	507	5.74	37.54	.38	.61
Belgium	101	378	11.04	38.57	.88	.59
Denmark	5	205	1.09	40.51	.09	.59
Canada	75	880	4.21	38.54	.19	.58
New Zealand	b	66	b	21.26	b	.52
Germany	223	1,689	4.18	27.32	.31	.40
United Kingdom	407	863	7.75	15.40	.56	.38
United States	2,702	4,007	14.96	18.76	.53	.26
Japan	105	1,148	1.13	10.26	.24	.24
Finland	c	48	c	10.20	c	.19
Switzerland	4	104	.75	16.24	.04	.19
Austria	3[d]	64	.43[d]	8.50	.04[d]	.17
Italy	77	182	1.56	3.26	.22	.11
Portugal	37	e	4.15	e	1.45	e

[a] Listed in percentage of GNP for 1975 in accordance with the 1975 ODA (Official Development Assistance).

[b] New Zealand joined the DAC in 1973; ODA figures for 1960 are not available.

[c] Finland joined the DAC in 1975; ODA figures for 1960 are not available.

[d] This figure refers to 1961.

[e] Portugal withdrew from the DAC in October 1974; figures for 1975 are not available.

Sources: The above table is based on the report by the chairman of the Development Assistance Committee, *Development Cooperation, 1971 Review* (Paris, OECD, 1971), pp. 165 and 175; Report by the chairman of the Development Assistance Committee, *Development Cooperation, 1976 Review* (Paris, OECD, 1976), Tables 2 and 44; and the United Nations Department of Economic and Social Affairs, *Demographic Yearbook*, 1961, table 4, pp. 126-37.

Bibliography

Listed below are some very useful works complementary to those quoted in the text.

AMIN, S. *Le Développement inégal*. Paris, Ed. de Minuit, 1973.

ANGELOPOULOS, A. *Pour une nouvelle politique du développement international*. Paris, PUF, 1976.

"L'Argent", La NEF, No. 65, juillet-août-septembre 1977.

AUSTRUY, J. *Le Scandale du développement*. Paris, M. Rivière, 1965.

BAIROCH, P. *Le Tiers Monde dans l'impasse*. Paris, Gallimard, 1971.

BETTELHEIM, C. *Planification et croissance accélérée*. Paris, F. Maspero, 1964.

BRESSON, Y. *Le Capital temps, pouvoir, répartition et inégalités*. Paris, Calmann-Lévy, 1977.

COLE, J. *The poor of the earth*. London, Macmillan, 1976.

CORNELIUS, W. A., TRUEBOLD, F. M. *Urbanization and inequality; the political economy of urban and rural development in Latin America*. Beverley Hills, Calif., Sage Publications, 1976.

Dag Hammarskjöld Foundation. *What now? Report prepared on the occasion of the seventh special session of the United Nations General Assembly*. Uppsala, 1975.

DAMACHI, U. G., ROUTH, G., ALI-TAHA, A.-R. E. *Development paths in Africa and China*. London, Macmillan, 1976.

"Du bien-être", ZOMAR, No. 7, septembre-octobre 1977. (Sté coopérative ZOMAR, case postale, CH 2501, Bienne, Suisse.)

ERB, G. F., KALLAB, V., eds. *Beyond dependency: the developing world speaks out*. Washington, Overseas Development Council, 1975.

"L'Essai de dialogue Nord-Sud: une année de négociations difficiles." Le Monde, 21 déc. 1976, p. 18.

ESSEKS and others. *L'Afrique de l'indépendance politique à l'indépendance économique*. Paris, Maspero, 1975.

FALKOWSKI, M. *Les Problèmes de la croissance du tiers monde vus par les économistes des pays socialistes*. Paris, Payot, 1968.

FURTADO, C. *La Formation économique du Brésil, de l'époque coloniale aux temps modernes*. Paris, Mouton, 1972.

GALTUNG, J. *The Lomé Convention and neo-colonialism*. Oslo, University of Oslo, 1975.

GENDARME, R. *La Pauvreté des nations*. 2e éd. Paris, Cujas, 1973.

HENRY, P.-M., BIROU, A. *Pour un autre développement*. Paris, PUF, 1976.

HERMASSI, E. *Etat et société au Maghreb*. Paris, Anthropos, 1975.

HERRERA, A. O. *Un Monde pour tous*. Ouvrage collectif, réalisé sous les auspices de la Fondation Bariloche. Paris, PUF, 1977.

177

HIRSCHMAN, A. *Controversia sobre Latinoamérica.* Buenos Aires, Ed. del Instituto, 1963.

ILLICH, I. *Le Chômage créateur.* Paris, Seuil, 1977.

International Institute for Labour Studies. "Report of the World Symposium on the Social Implications of a New International Economic Order." *Labour and society,* Vol. 1, Nos. 3-4, July-Oct. 1976.

JAN, M. *La Vie Chinoise.* Paris, PUF, 1976.

LACOSTE, Y. *Géographie du sous-développement.* Paris, PUF, 1965.

LARAOUI, A. *L'Idéologie arabe contemporaine.* Paris, Maspero, 1977.

LEBRET, L.-J. *Dynamique concrète du développement.* Paris, Ed. Ouvrières, 1961.

LEONTIEF, W. and others. *The future of the world economy.* New York, Oxford University Press, 1977.

MOLLAT, M. *Etudes sur l'histoire de la pauvreté.* Paris, Publications de la Sorbonne, 1974.

MOREHOUSE, W., SIGURDSON, J. *Science, technology and poverty: the issues underlying the 1979 World Conference on Science and Technology for Development.* Lund, Sweden, Lund University, 1977.

MORGAN, T., SPOELSTRA, N., eds. *Economic interdependence in Southeast Asia.* London, University of Wisconsin Press, 1969.

MYRDAL, G. *Le Défi du monde pauvre.* Paris, Gallimard, 1971.

"Le Mythe du développement." Collectif sous la direction de Candido Mendes. Paris, Ed. du Seuil, *Esprit,* 1977.

NAIDU, S. B. *La Voie indienne du développement.* Paris, Ed. Ouvrières, 1971.

NANA-SINKAM, S. *Pays candidats au processus de développement: capacité d'absorption, assistance extérieure et modèles de croissance économique.* Paris, Mouton, 1975.

PANG, Th. *Les Communes populaires rurales en Chine.* Cahiers de l'Institut des sciences économiques et sociales, No. 18, Ed. Universitaires de Fribourg, 1967.

REGAMEY, P. R. *Pauvreté chrétienne et construction du monde.* Paris, Ed. du Cerf, 1968.

REMILI, A. *Tiers monde et émergence d'un nouvel ordre économique international.* Alger, Office des publications universitaires, 1976.

Reshaping the international order: a report to the Club of Rome. Coordinated by Jan Tinbergen. New York, E. Dutton, 1976.

ROY, M.-P. "La Convention de Lomé—CEE-Pays d'Afrique, des Caraïbes et du Pacifique—Amorce d'un nouvel ordre économique international." *Notes et études documentaires,* Nos. 4313-4315, 1976.

SAUVY, A. *L'Economie du diable.* Paris, Calmann-Lévy, 1976.

SCHUMACHER, E. F. *Small is beautiful: a study of economics as if people mattered.* London, Blond and Briggs, 1973.

TINBERGEN, J. *Politique économique et optimum social.* Paris, Optima, 1972.

TOYNBEE, A. J., IKEDA, D. *The Toynbee-Ikeda dialogue.* Tokyo, Kodansha, 1976.

ZEVIN, L. Z. *Economic co-operation of socialist and developing countries: new trends.* Moscow, USSR Academy of Sciences, 1976.

Index of Names

Abdesselam, B. 132
Abu Thar El Ghafair 7
Achard, P. 13 n
Ahidjo, A. 43
Alain 98
Al Khatabi 145
Amin, S. 30, 55
Aquinas, Th. 5 n
Archimedes 124
Aristotle 53
Aron, Raymond 20
Assisi, F. d' 5
Attali, J. 15, 23
Aubert, C. 78 n
Augustine (Saint) 137
Aventurin, E. 112 n

Baader-Meinhof (Group) 152
Bacon, Fr. 54
Bairoch, P. 25, 49
Bandolo, H. 132 n
Beart, G. 23
Bemba, S. 32
Benevides Pinho, D. 120
Ben Maimon, M. (Maimonides) 3, 4
Berlinguer, E. 24
Bernard, C. 55
Berque, J. 30
Berthelot, Y. 54
Bettelheim, Ch. 79 n
Beveridge, A. 93
Biedermann, K. 8
Blanchard, F. 63 n, 148 n, 167
Blardone, G. 103 n
Bogaert, M. v. d. 81 n
Boileau 92 n
Boissonnat, J. 87 n
Bono, O. 36
Borremans, V. 72 n

Bosquet, M. 16 n
Bossuet 5
Boumedienne, H. 118, 135
Brandt (Commission) 159
Brettveld, H. 72 n
Brezhnev, L. 128
Brooklin, M. 73
Broyelle, C. and J. 24
Bruce-Briggs, B. 152 n
Brzezinski, Z. 112, 113

Carlyle, Th. 8
Carter, J. 113, 147
Castel, M. 75
Castro, J. de 40, 66, 67
Catiline 25
Césaire, A. 26, 88, 139
Chauvenet, A. 13 n
Cheysson, C. 161
Cicero 25
Closets, F. de 87 n
Copernicus, N. 55
Corea, G. 162
Coulomb (Prof.) 72

Dadié, B. 31
Delors, J. 129
Descartes, R. 52
Desroche, H. 119
Diawara, M. 88 n
Díaz Míron, S. 90
Diogenes 52
Diop, B. 26
Diouf, M. 165
Dovlo, F. 67, 68 n
Drouin, P. 166
Dulles, F. 147
Dumont, R. 10, 14, 25, 108 n
Dupuy, J.-P. 13 n

179

Index of Names